CREATIVITY

In Creativity as Co-Therapist, experienced psychotherapist and creativity expert, Lisa Ruth Mitchell, bridges the gap between theoretical knowledge and therapeutic application by teaching psychotherapists of all backgrounds to see therapy as their art form. Readers are guided through the five stages of the creative process to help them understand the complexities of approaching their work creatively and to effectively identify areas in which they tend to get stuck when working with clients. Along the way workbook assignments, case studies, personal stories, and hands-on art invitations will inspire the reader to think outside the box and build the creative muscles that hold the key to enlivening their work.

Lisa Ruth Mitchell, LMFT, LPC, ATR, veteran art therapist with over twenty years of clinical experience, runs the Art Therapy Studio in Sacramento, California. Through her website, InnerCanvas, she writes, teaches, and facilitates retreats for therapists showing them how to harness the power of creativity and facilitate individualized handcrafted therapy sessions.

CREATIVITY AS CO-THERAPIST

THE PRACTITIONER'S GUIDE TO THE ART OF PSYCHOTHERAPY

Lisa Ruth Mitchell

Routledge
Taylor & Francis Group

NEW YORK AND LONDON

First published 2016
by Routledge
711 Third Avenue, New York, NY 10017

and by Routledge
2 Park Square, Milton Park, Abingdon, Oxon, OX14 4RN

Routledge is an imprint of the Taylor & Francis Group, an informa business

© 2016 Lisa Ruth Mitchell

Library of Congress Cataloging in Publication Data
Names: Mitchell, Lisa Ruth, author.
Title: Creativity as co-therapist : the practitioner's guide to the art of
psychotherapy / by Lisa Ruth Mitchell.
Description: New York, NY : Routledge, 2016.
Includes bibliographical references and index.
Identifiers: LCCN 2015034068 | ISBN 9781138852747 (hbk : alk. paper)
| ISBN 9781138852730 (pbk : alk. paper) | ISBN 9781315723327 (ebk)
Subjects: LCSH: Art therapy. | Therapist and patient. | Creative ability.
Classification: LCC RC489.A7 .M58 2016
DDC 616.89/1656–dc23
LC record available at http://lccn.loc.gov/2015034068

ISBN: 978-1-138-85274-7 (hbk)
ISBN: 978-1-138-85273-0 (pbk)
ISBN: 978-1-315-72332-7 (ebk)

Typeset in Baskerville
by Out of House Publishing

For Wilfred Mitchell (1907–1988)
and Ruth Mitchell (1908–1992)
If only you could know the thread of you I carry forward.

CONTENTS

The plate section falls between pages 130 *and* 131

PROLOGUE

Finding Beauty

I slid down the wall outside the padded room and found a seat on the cold linoleum, desperately trying to send soothing thoughts to the agitated captive within. All I could hear were animal growls, agonizing wails, and violent thumps as they migrated through the cracked seal that locked the cell door. He didn't know I was there at the hospital, or that I was on duty as a mental health investigator. He probably didn't even know where he was or why he had been 5150ed. The nurses explained he had been walking all night and was picked up by the police after refusing to leave the median strip that divided the busy street in front of the concert hall.

The night before, I had sat still, all ears, letting his elegant piano notes wash over me. I had been entranced by his passion. His graceful hands grabbed complex chords as his eyes pierced the dark stage. His ability to communicate emotion through his music was stunning, and I felt sparked by inspiration. It was a feeling I hadn't experienced in long while. When I left the hall, tingling with appreciation, I felt I could run all the way home and still have energy to paint a masterpiece. He was beauty in action.

And now he was beauty caged. The sounds that came from within the solitary confinement room were not magical—they were painful. And I felt helpless. Until this moment, I had never witnessed mental illness this close.

I was 22 years old, fresh out of college in my first real job. The public defenders with whom I worked thought my fascination with the legal services we provided to people with mental illness was strange. Graduation briefcase slung over my shoulder, weighted down with case files, I would arrive at the local locked facilities and interview patients to make sure their rights weren't being violated, or listen intently to patients who had requested a writ in protest of their involuntary holds. I was innocent and young, but unlike others in my office, I was not at all repelled.

But this day, the day that Jonathan, the brilliant concert pianist, was being held in solitary—pacing, wailing, hitting the door—was an eye opener. His parents had called the public defenders' office, and the office had sent me to the hospital. I sat in the cold hallway for hours. The staff there wouldn't let me talk to him. They wouldn't listen to me when I tried to tell them who he was. I didn't feel like an efficient investigator. I didn't feel I could do anything at all.

Then I remembered his beauty—his magic—his music. I began to hum the Beethoven sonata that he'd played the night before, the same piece that had brought tears to my eyes. I knew every note because it had been my mother's most practiced piece from my childhood. She lent me the notes; he lent me the memory of his passion. And I hummed.

After a few minutes, the wails had quieted to whimpers. I heard him fall against the floor into stillness, the violent thumping no longer an accompaniment to my Beethoven hum. Though he and I sat with a wall between us, I felt joined with him and with my mother in our shared appreciation for the beauty of music. Without thinking, I stopped a nurse who was walking by and told him that it was urgent: he had to let the piano player out. He had to let him play. The nurse started to protest, but for some divine reason acquiesced.

Together we led Jonathan to the clumsy piano that sat in the community room. He sat down to play, and for the second time in 24 hours, I let the inspiration wash over me. He played Beethoven and he came back to himself. I sat on the ratty vinyl couch tuned to all that he had to say. His beauty was in action again.

That was when my mission was born. I realized at that moment that I was not an advocate for indigent defendants or an investigator for do-good lawyers and their impoverished clients. I was an advocate for art. I recognized that I was a junkie of sorts, looking for a fix of creativity even in places where it might not appear. I could draw it out, celebrate it, and set it free. And when I connected others with their artful beauty, healing happened over and over again.

I came to the field of art therapy with the mission to find beauty. My understanding about the value of creative expression in the context of a therapeutic relationship has evolved and deepened over the last 25 years. The beauty that I witness with my clients on a daily basis emerges from the experience of inviting the creative process into session over and over again. For me, it's not about the finished product but about the collaboration between client and therapist. Jonathan and I started our collaboration despite the barrier of a locked door, and it continued as he spoke through his piano music. The art unfolds and the relationship deepens.

So, today, while I carefully choose art invitations to help facilitate transformative experiences for my clients, I never lose sight of the true beauty of this work: the handcrafted nature of the healing relationship. The therapeutic relationship, like every other creative endeavor, relies on the process rather than the product. The very essence of healing and change stems from the process of making an artful connection with our clients, which is as specific and unique as any work of art. I believe that all therapists have the inherent drive to reach in and help turn on the shining brilliance of each person with whom we work. This book was written to help therapists and healing professionals understand the creative process and how it applies in our work, and celebrate what can happen when we trust it to guide us in our therapeutic relationships.

Dear Reader,

This book is not an instructional manual about how to use art in therapy. It doesn't walk you through a clinical protocol for treating specific disorders. It doesn't provide you with evidence-based practice techniques that will ensure that you fit into a standard of care. There are plenty of books like that. They are good and necessary.

This book picks up where those books left off. This book is about knowing ourselves as artists. It's about the internal states that we need to be aware of—that we have to live and embrace—in order for our work to be artful. When we are artists and our work is artful, we give ourselves and our clients permission to let doubt and anxiety and inspiration be part of the process of change. We become modern guides, real and courageous, who can walk beside our clients and step outside the comfort zone right along with them.

When you are an artist, you work without a step-by-step plan. The emotional intensity is sometimes overwhelming. But you are not bored, you are not numb, and, best of all, you are not drained. You are revitalized and occasionally stunned by the beauty you find in the process. I wish this for you because it is what our work is all about. It is what heals, what is beautiful, and what creates change.

My understanding of the creative process has developed over the last 20 years, having worked variously as a wraparound worker with low-income families, a caseworker with juvenile sex offenders, an art therapist for homeless teens, and now in my private practice with adults and adolescents. For the last decade as a consultant and workshop leader, I have also had the privilege of routinely witnessing the wide-eyed, heart-quickening excitement that arrives when a therapist views her work as an art form. This way of seeing comes as a relief. The fear of making a mistake gives way to the excitement of trying something new. Passion and curiosity peek out from under the tedium of repetition. It is a connection to something besides the pursuit of knowledge and skills that is emphasized in our training. In fact, it's a reconnection of sorts. When we see our work as art, we can see therapy as an act of love.

I truly believe that this is why many of us became therapists in the first place. I have heard many touching stories from therapists about that pivotal moment when at some point, they became aware of the rich potential of human connection. We fall in love with that potential, and we want to feel it and share it with others. My moment of awareness came while humming Beethoven and leaning against the door of that padded room in the psych ward. Can you remember your moment? Can you remember what it felt like to experience the intensity of this kind of love?

When all is said and done, this book is an invitation to you. I invite you to read the stories and make the art, to grapple with your creative process and embrace it as a thread that weaves through all things personal and professional. And most of all, I invite you to fall back in love with yourself and your work.

Yours,
Lisa Ruth Mitchell

ACKNOWLEDGMENTS

I want to acknowledge the following people for their support and collaboration. Greg Hudson often tells people I'm the most determined person he knows. Truth be told, my determination would go nowhere without his support. He is my number one art patron, my partner, and, most of all, my love. As my editor, Gwyn Fallbrooke provided the perfect blend of support and challenge. She was extraordinary in her ability to help me refine my message through her clear structure and enthusiasm. I couldn't have written this book without her. I want to acknowledge Chris Teja, whose editorial eye found me and allowed me to write exactly what I wanted. Austen Redinger lent his creative process to make the awesome illustrations. Rich Simon started this whole project by initiating me into the world of professional writing. And my coaches, Andrea J. Lee and Lynn Grodzki, helped me discern what it is I love and how to best bring it into the world. Nina Denninger told me in no uncertain terms that I wanted to be an art therapist, which set me on the perfect career and life path. Susan Orr mentored me along that path. The works of Jeffery Kottler, Jon Carlson, Robert Akeret, and Irvin Yalom inspired me to write from a therapist's perspective. The therapists from all over the world who I've had the privilege of teaching online and in my own studio have helped me see and understand the creative process in action. And my clients—my dear clients—have given me decades of experience with the art of relationship and healing. Our art goes way beyond words and weaves a creative thread that will span generations to come. It has been a privilege to create with each and every one of them.

I also want to say thank you to my kids, Mitch, Sam, and Ruth; my mother, Sharon Eakes; and my dear friends (too many to list). You have each inspired me in profound ways. Your support and love are what I cherish most.

INTRODUCTION

Who this Book is For

This book easily fits on the shelves with other art therapy texts, but I'd rather it lived on a shelf marked "The Art of Therapy." This book will be helpful for any therapist who wants to infuse his or her practice with creativity, regardless of theoretical approach or orientation. This book is for art therapists, trauma therapists, grief counselors, palliative care workers, solution-focused therapists, cognitive behavioral therapists, psychologists, counselors, social workers, and any other type of helping professional who would like to partner with their creativity and learn to apply what they already know in exciting and effective ways.

How this Book Works

Julia Cameron's seminal book, *The Artist's Way* (1992), has become an invaluable guide for millions of readers to living an artist's life. My editor Chris Teja has described *Creativity as Co-Therapist* as *The Artist's Way* for therapists. Like Cameron, I believe that everyone is an artist and that creative expression is the natural direction of life. In this book, I apply this same principle to our work as therapists and aim to help us recover our creativity, become more artful in forming healing relationships, and provide handcrafted therapy for our clients. In addition to helping readers understand the creative process, this book is meant to help therapists see themselves as artists in their own right. And, as Cameron does in her book, I offer concrete activities and questions designed to facilitate this discovery.

Because it might be a new way of thinking, Part I of this book explains how I have come to think about the therapeutic process as a creative process. Part II contains a Creativity Assessment and some important guidelines for relating to art and art making. In each of the subsequent chapters, I describe the five stages of the creative process and what it takes to navigate them. The first stage, Incubating, invites us to think about clients outside of session and to brainstorm ideas about our work. Incubating is a vacation from analyzing, and requires permissiveness and openness to information that may seem unrelated to our clients' issues. Initial Idea, the second stage, asks us to distill our ideas and find a clear sense of how we will proceed. It is the crystallization of a starting point for our work with each client in each session. The third stage, Diving In, is marked by the act of implementing the Initial Idea. This stage can be tricky as it invites us to act on our Initial Idea without being certain of the outcome. Diving In is often accompanied by risk and the potentially uncomfortable anxiety that accompanies it. The fourth stage, Flexible Commitment, requires that we be willing to treat mistakes as opportunities and be nimble in our thoughts. In this stage, we are reminded of the importance of a collaborative stance with our clients. Finally, in the fifth stage of the creative process, we are in Flow. Here, we feel a sense of effortlessness. Our sense of time and emphasis on understanding are secondary to feelings of timelessness, connectedness, and transcendence.

I have included a variety of stories from my own life and work experiences in this book. The case studies, childhood experiences, and peak moments with clients are all shared with the intent to shine a light on the varied ways that the creative process looks and feels.

With this book, I am extending an invitation for permissiveness and risk taking—aspects of the creative process—to become a regular part of our work. In so doing, I am not inviting a free-for-all where we abandon ethics and foundational training. We still need to pay attention to the boundaries of the therapeutic relationship and whether or not our clients are benefiting from our work. Some of my stories include incidents that may be considered outside the norm. I believe that when we usher clients into new experiences, we have to be open to new experiences ourselves, and sometimes that means trying things that have not been done before. I'm excited to share some of these "out-of-the-box" experiences that I have had with clients. I'm also happy to share some of the wonderful moments I have witnessed as a result of working with other therapists in my workshops and retreats.

In keeping with our profession's ethical standards, I have taken great measures to preserve client anonymity. All of the client stories are altered and/or fictionalized composites to protect client rights. Many of the moments are so unique that they are impossible to disguise without obliterating the magic. For this reason, I have made sure to get permission from each client to tell our story and share it here.

For each of the five stages of the creative process, I offer a set of journaling questions and art invitations. There is a huge variety here as well. Some art invitations are simple and require only drawing paper and markers or crayons. Others are quite complex. Time is always an issue, and we all struggle with not having enough of it. I fully appreciate the temptation to simply read this book's contents, without doing any accompanying art, in an attempt to understand the concept of the creative process and how it parallels the therapeutic process. But I encourage you to make time and dive in to the art invitations. The doing of them is key; they provide you with the necessary practice that will help you grasp the felt sense experience of seeing your work as an art form. The art invitations are also a way to experience creativity in another medium besides therapy and to provide a way to practice and develop trust in all mediums. Many of the art activities have accompanying videos that can be accessed on my site at www.innercanvas.com/creativity-cotherapist. Please feel free to visit there for further explanations, demonstration, and inspiration.

Our art mediums need one another—visual art, music, dance, writing, theatre. Natalie Goldberg, writer, painter, and muse to writers all over the world, talks about this relationship in her book *Living Color* (2014). Her writing and painting were so intertwined that when she gave up painting in order to have more time to write, she says: "I cut off the underground stream of mayhem, joy, nonsense, absurdity. Painting was what continually kept those ducts clean and open, because I never took painting seriously. Without painting, sludge gathered at the mouth of the river and eventually clogged any flow."

I think this is true of our work as therapists. In my courses and retreats, I hear participants celebrate the new understanding that when we set aside time for our creative work in other areas—for example, visual art—our creative work as therapists feels cleaner and is filled with a greater sense of flow. I hope this provides some incentive to try all of the art invitations. And if your sense of yourself as an artist is tenuous or nonexistent, the next chapters will offer some heartening encouragement and advice for proceeding.

Part I

THE ART OF THERAPY

1

THE THERAPEUTIC PROCESS
IS A CREATIVE PROCESS

The Role of Mistakes

As an intern with a dual degree in art therapy and counseling, I worked hard to learn to do things the "right" way. Early on, I started filling a recipe box that matched specific art therapy techniques with their corresponding treatment goals. I rehearsed how to word brief therapy questions and practiced guided visualization scripts. My emphasis on finding the right tool or technique was my yardstick. If I used the right one, I was doing well. If I couldn't figure out what kind of art activity to ask the client to do or what specific concept to teach, I felt overwhelmed and uncomfortable. I agonized over mistakes and couldn't wait for the day when I felt experienced enough to feel like I knew what I was doing. The message that I had taken away from my graduate program was decidedly weighted with the need for certainty. I coveted therapeutic moments of comfort and proficiency, where I didn't waver, falter, or dabble with not-knowing. And as a result, I strived to know my theories inside and out, to apply them with perfection, and to avoid errors at all cost.

I took this same approach with me into my oral exam, the second test on the road to Marriage, Family, and Child Counselor (MFCC) licensure in California. It had a widely criticized and mysterious reputation, but every intern who wanted to be licensed had to train to answer 12 questions about a clinical vignette for a panel of three licensed therapists. Knowing that the pass rate hovered below 40 percent, I had trained for months and created a complex grid system to make sure that I covered all of the criteria for any possible vignette I was given.

On the day of my test, I held my nerves in check while sitting in the "holding room." I tried to breathe as I stood in the elevator going up to the exam room (a hotel room with the bed removed). I read the vignette, took my notes, and started to answer questions. I was doing fine until a stone-faced examiner asked me question six. I realized in that moment that I had already answered this question and had mixed it up for question four. I knew that if I didn't go back and talk about the answer for question four, I would fail. All of the content was necessary to pass. I had made a mistake, and I didn't know how to get out of it. So I just told them, red-faced. "I've made a mistake. I think I answered this question already. I must have mixed the questions up and misheard what you asked for number four. I'm sorry. Would it be okay if I went back and talked about question four instead?" I was sure I had failed right then.

One examiner smiled, or maybe smirked. The examiner next to him said, "You can say whatever you want." I couldn't read his tone. It was neutral, matter-of-fact, and perhaps a bit impatient.

So I launched into my answer for question four. I covered the content well enough and was able to get through the rest of the exam without crying. My mistake was evidence that I was a terrible listener. I hadn't been careful enough. They would think I didn't have the skills it took to be a therapist. During the six weeks I waited to receive my test results, I had decided that I couldn't go through the exam a second time. I started to make backup plans and imagined myself becoming a preschool teacher or a receptionist in a hair salon.

The day that I received my letter saying I had passed and was officially a licensed MFCC, I was stunned. How could they pass me after that mistake? I was grateful and relieved, but didn't understand. I called a colleague of mine who had sat on oral exam panels to ask him what he thought. Why had they passed someone who messed up like that? He told me a profound truth. "It's not about answering the questions perfectly," he said. "The content is important, but the real test is in how you are able to hold yourself in that level of stress and how well you recover from the mistakes. It is a good thing that you made a mistake and that you recovered from it. That showed them a vital part of what will make you a successful therapist."

I was grateful for my colleague's comments, but I didn't fully take his message to heart. I thought he was being nice and reframing my mistake just to make me feel better. So it is no surprise that I continued to strive for certainty in knowing what I was doing. I wanted the security of knowing that I could deliver my services without making a mistake.

I remember a particularly painful period in 2002, during which I got my Eye Movement Desensitization and Reprocessing (EMDR) certificate and was training with Bruce Ecker to master his Depth-Oriented Brief Therapy (now Coherence Therapy) model. I had the idea that this excellent set of skills was going to eliminate my self-doubt and that my work with clients was going to become easier. I thought knowledge would give me a formula that would take away the uncertainty and finally make me feel secure in my role as therapist. I worked very hard at applying the protocols. I perfected the wording. I consulted and refined. But during a gathering of therapist friends, I found myself in tears because I realized I was not feeling more proficient; instead, I was feeling robotic and inauthentic, trapped at an assembly line of client issues. While I believed I was doing adequate work, I wasn't being artful. In my endeavor to eliminate uncertainty, I had killed my creativity. I had sold out and, in the process, lost a part of myself that had brought me to the work in the first place.

Scott Miller reintroduced me to this quandary in a 2007 meeting for chapter leaders of the California Association of Marriage and Family Therapists. In his talk, Miller passionately discouraged his colleagues from allowing a state of proficiency to lull us into mediocrity. He called our therapist culture error-phobic and pointed out that this effort to avoid mistakes had fueled a standardization of our practices. He shot down our profession's assumption that we get better the longer we practice our craft, and instead informed us that we had successfully achieved automaticity and an inflated sense of confidence rather than actual excellence in the field.

"Our profession is the only one that gives you five or six chances to feel like a failure every day," he told us. I was relieved and amused. Here I'd been, struggling to achieve proficiency in order to be more effective, only to be swept under by the assembly-line approach Miller was describing.

He offered another approach at this meeting. The most successful therapists, he said, were actually the ones who took an *error-centric* approach, who focused on what wasn't going right, who treated mistakes as opportunities, and who admitted that they didn't always have the answer. They were the ones who were in fact better than average.

Scott Miller's talk was the beginning of my realization that the therapeutic process was actually a creative process. I began to reflect on my lifelong experience as an artist and how I had learned firsthand the importance of mistakes in the creative process. I have been a dabbling artist ever since I can remember; I've logged a lot of studio time, both before and after I became a therapist. I realized that the joy and spontaneity that my art making had given me were precisely due to the fact that I had never tried to become proficient. I had always rejected evaluation of the end product and instead emphasized the degree of creative expression and experimentation during the process. Many of the paintings and sculptures I had created over the years relied on the new ideas I had discovered in the course of making a "mistake." I much preferred trying something totally new, something about which I had no way of predicting the outcome, over and above a paint-by-numbers kit. So I started to take Scott Miller's invitation seriously, to bring my error-centric artist's culture into my work as a therapist, and aimed to abandon my error-phobic ways.

Think of the training that you have received. In supervision, did your supervisor give you the latitude to make mistakes?

Have you ever had the privilege of watching a training video where a master therapist modeled what it looked like when things were not going right? Were you taught to open yourself to a collaborative stance with your client and invite feedback that might make you feel vulnerable?

The result of an informal poll of therapists from my online classes shows how they react when things aren't going right. Eighty percent of them stated that they had doubts as to whether they were the right therapists for their clients. Instead of looking at the situation as an opportunity to try something new, they assumed that there was another therapist—probably more experienced—who would do better at the job than they could. Because we are taught to be error-phobic, we miss out on the error-centric creative process that could improve our resilience and ability to stay engaged and alive in our work.

Our creative process depends on us to make mistakes. Norcross's (2010) research confirms that a therapist's admitting to error actually enhances the therapeutic alliance. For both artists and therapists, what we do with mistakes is much more important than whether we make mistakes at all. When I began to see the therapeutic process as a creative process, I adopted this potent antidote against collapsing into self-doubt. I could see how considering myself an artist not only in sculpture and painting, but also in therapy, allowed me to be more present and build more engaging connections with my clients because I didn't have to be so careful about getting it "right."

Maslow (1959) helped me understand the relationship between creativity, errors, and the ability to create strong thera-peutic relationships in his essay, "Creativity in Self-Actualizing People." He wrote:

> When you are creative, you are more self-accepting than the average, less afraid of your own thoughts, and less afraid of being laughed at or disapproved of. You can let yourself be flooded by emotion and you waste less time and energy protecting yourself against yourself.
>
> (Maslow, 1959: p. 88)

As Maslow's quote suggests, when we are creative and embrace an error-centric approach to therapy, we are more likely to step out of the comfort zone of proficiency and try new ideas because we are not afraid to make mistakes. We know that mistakes are opportunities that lead us to new discoveries for ourselves and our clients. In the end, this leads to us become more creative, more self-actualized, more innovative, and, most importantly, better at doing our work.

The Role of a Collaborative Relationship

In *The Heart and Soul of Change: Delivering What Works in Therapy*, Duncan, Miller, Wampold, and Hubble (2010) report ground-breaking findings in their meta-analysis of evidence-based psychotherapy research. Their results subvert the idea that there exists a set of specific techniques and approaches for successful treatment of specific disorders, and instead concludes that there is one primary factor that predicts the success of therapy: the therapeutic relationship. This may be old news, but it is worth reiterating here. When encountering a difficult situation with a client, it is easy and tempting to soothe self-doubt with a ready-made protocol. I remember a particularly ridiculous cascade of professional despair when I decided I absolutely had to learn Acceptance and Commitment Therapy in one weekend. I was sure that if I watched all ten DVDs and mastered at least some of the language, I would have a way out of the stuck place in which I had found myself with my client. Learning new modalities and protocols is important, but depending on them to give us the answer is neither effective nor creative. In fact, as Norcross (2010) reports, "The small body of research indicates that the frequency and severity of ruptures are increased by rigid adherence to a treatment manual and an excessive number of transference interpretations." If we look to the relationship instead of to techniques, we immediately return to a collaborative stance with our clients. And when we collaborate, we do so not just with our clients but with our techniques and protocols as well.

This view that we are active collaborators in the creation of our art is not unfamiliar to art students. Ever since it opened in 1793, the Louvre has allowed, and even encouraged, artists to hone their skills by copying the masterpieces in its collections (Harriss, 2001). Cezanne, who came to the Louvre to copy Michelangelo, Rubens, and classical Greek and Roman statues, noted: "The Louvre is the book where we learn to read."

But why do artists flock to copy masters' paintings? It is not to be able to paint like the masters. Instead, they want to learn how the masters solved their artistic problems. They follow the footprints left in the form of the painting in order to learn how the master painter navigated the painting process. In this act of replication, the copier gleans a deeper experience with her own creative process. The master is not there telling the copier what to do each step of the way. The paintings invite the copier into a valuable experience of being an active participant in the process. The master supplies the guide and starting point; the real discovery comes from the collaboration between the copier and her own canvas.

Think of it. If you can imagine yourself trying to copy a master painting at the Louvre, it might be tempting to imagine that in order to copy well, you must figure out how the master applied the paint or used color or rendered a gesture. But this kind of effortful focus on the technical side blinds us from seeing ourselves as active participants in the painting process. We are so busy concentrating on the master painting that our contributions become much less important. But now I'd like you to imagine that you are there in the Louvre, and you discover that you absolutely adore what happens when you layer a veil of Titanium White over Phthalo Blue. While this may or may not be the exact combination that your master used in his painting, your adoration of your discovery causes you to become an active participant in your painting process. In this sense, there is true collaboration between you and your very own painting. A few more of these discoveries, and you are no longer concentrating on how the master painted his painting. Your emphasis becomes about you, your discovery process, and the relationship you establish with your emerging painting.

Around the same time that I heard Scott Miller speak about mistakes, I noticed my internal emphasis on technique mastery diminishing; instead, I began to hone in on moments during a session when I delighted at the original application of an intervention or spontaneously made something up to suit the situation. These were moments when I could see my own creative process coming to light. I could see myself as an active participant in the therapeutic relationship because I was no longer copying and concentrating so hard on re-creating the master's work. This vibrant awareness is what this book is aimed at helping therapists to cultivate.

In my workshops, I love inviting therapists to identify special moments they have experienced with specific clients. This moment can be a time when a client turned a corner in treatment; when the therapist or the client had a lightning-bolt insight that changed everything; or when the therapist felt particularly entranced by the therapeutic process. It doesn't matter if it is a shared moment in which both therapist and client have checked in to validate the significance of the experience. It just matters if something profound happened—something special and memorable.

Every therapist has moments like these, and it turns out that we all keep them in our back pockets for rainy days. They are like little charms that give us a boost when we need one. Take a minute to think about one of your special moments. Tell yourself the story. Walk yourself through the experience. What was it like?

Much of the time, when I ask therapists to describe the moment, they talk about what the client did. They can narrate in great detail what happened as their eyes glaze over with that sweet sense of satisfaction. Sometimes therapists will talk about what specific technique they decided to use. "I asked my client to put his mother in the empty chair." "I walked her through a guided visualization that put her in touch with her resource."

"I asked her to draw her anxiety as a monster." Other times, therapists will say, "I don't know what happened. It was magical." These kinds of comments indicate that they are not taking into account who they were in that moment. Instead, they are focusing on what they could or couldn't replicate—a technique, a directive, a phrase. And if they can't identify anything specific, they chalk it up to magic.

Many aspects of our field have contributed to this tendency for therapists to erase themselves from the creative collaboration that transpires with clients. For instance, we are trained to become well versed in the many aspects of reading our own feelings in order to better understand what our clients may be feeling. Projective identification and countertransference are useful concepts that can help us understand what might be going on, and yet they require us to mine our emotional reactions and melt ourselves into the background in order to better serve our clients.

When I ask therapists to take one of those special moments and to really look at what they did to help create that moment with a client, they often wake up to a discovery much like that of the copier at the Louvre. They see themselves as direct contributors to the moment, and can say, for example, "I let myself get vulnerable and trust." "I allowed more quiet than is normally comfortable." "I strayed from my protocol because my gut told me to share a personal story." Invariably, what the therapist did to help create those moments was not outlined in a technique or methodology. Instead it was based on a shift of focus from product to process; from technique to relationship; from therapy as something we do *to* a client to therapy as something we do *with* a client.

Then, and only then, can we focus on the most important factor determining the outcome of therapy: the creation of a collaborative relationship. With this focus, the process becomes an artful one, with both therapist and client working together as artists to connect and to create change.

The Role of Anxiety and Doubt

Around the same time that Scott Miller's lecture offered me a glimpse into how the therapeutic process is a creative process, Orlinksy and Rønnestad's research on the professional development of nearly 5,000 psychotherapists strengthened the link between the work of artists and the work of therapists. It didn't surprise me that 70 to 80 percent of the therapists they polled reported having had recent experiences of Flow feelings; I had felt them myself at times. These Flow feelings were described as "intense absorption, finely calibrated responsiveness, and keenly felt satisfaction." Specifically, 80 percent of the therapists felt stimulated, 80 percent felt engrossed, 79 percent felt inspired, and 70 percent felt challenged. But it occurred to me that these are the same feelings I and many of my artist friends have while we engage in our creative process. That was the first parallel I recognized between the therapeutic process and art making.

The second parallel was more surprising. For the psychotherapists in Orlinksy and Rønnestad's research, Boredom and Anxiety were not rare experiences. A clear majority of therapists felt occasionally pressured (74 percent), overwhelmed (64 percent), anxious (64 percent), and trapped (63 percent). Interestingly, the research found that "therapists can perceive and feel that they are helping their patients, even while experiencing the stressfulness of therapeutic work" (Orlinksy and Rønnestad, 2005: p. 44). The seemingly negative feeling of Anxiety didn't stop these therapists from experiencing Flow. In fact, they found that many of these therapists experienced these opposing feelings, Anxiety and Flow, within the same session.

This research into the experience of psychotherapists also described the very experience I had had as an artist. Indeed, while I had reveled in the Flow feelings, I had also come to recognize that anxiety and overwhelm, among other unpleasant emotions, are hallmarks of a successful creative process.

Artists dance with anxiety. They cultivate specific relationships with their inner critic and learn not to let their creative process be halted by difficult feelings. Therapists do this, too! When I realized this parallel, I couldn't help but think of various ways in which the creative process asks us to embrace the difficult feelings. If an artist stops painting every time fear rears its ugly head, she will never finish a painting. If a writer can't muster the courage to face a disastrous first draft, the novel will never get written. If a therapist collapses into doubt and failure, the session will screech to a stop and the client won't benefit.

In this book, we will look at anxiety's role in the creative process. When we learn that anxiety isn't automatically a warning sign of danger, but rather a sign of newness, we don't have to get stuck. And as we practice partnering with our creative process, we are able to reflect on times when anxiety didn't stop us in our creative tracks but instead spurred us on to make incredible things happen. We will see how the creative process utilizes doubt and uncertainty and allows us to embrace the unknown so that we are fully engaged with our clients and highly attuned to their feedback.

Summary

We have seen the positive role that mistakes have in both the creative process and the therapeutic process. Research tells us that what we do with a mistake is actually more important than the mistake we've made. We have also explored the idea that using an empirically validated therapeutic approach is not the most important factor in determining a successful outcome in therapy. Instead, the therapist's ability to forge a collaborative relationship with the client and to show up as an authentic person in the here-and-now is more essential. Finally, we have seen that anxiety does not have to interrupt the process and can even be seen as a signal that something new is about to happen.

In the chapters to follow, we will dive in further to these concepts and unpack the creative process to see and experience their specific subtleties. But I would like to end this chapter with one last thought.

In *The Icarus Deception*, Seth Godin, an expert on the creative process and its application to our work, says: "We get better at what we practice" (2012: Part Five, Section 41). In light of the points we have touched on so far, what are you practicing? Are you practicing being a good direction follower or a good masterpiece copier? Are you practicing not making mistakes? Are you practicing fitting into a specific theoretical approach? Are you trying to be like someone other than yourself?

Now, what would you like to practice instead? If you could get better at something else, what would you practice? How about recovering from mistakes, or treating mistakes as opportunities? Maybe you'd like to practice showing up as a real, authentic person to whom your clients can relate?

When we make creativity our co-therapist, we look at the therapeutic process differently. We become more three-dimensional to ourselves and to our clients. We become spontaneous and alive, riveting and entertaining, and our work is more personal and handcrafted for each unique client. In large part, we learn to accept ourselves, which invites us to follow our own voice and teach our clients, through our modeling, to do the same. When we do this, we are likely to find many unexpected treasures along the way.

And so I offer another story.

Unexpected Treasures

For several weeks I had been creating a tiny mountain of heart rocks on my husband's desk. Finding heart rocks has always been a thing of mine. Whether I was at the river, the beach, or at the bottom of the Grand Canyon, I'd be walking along minding my own business and a heart shape would invite me to stop, pick it up, and slip it into my pocket. In 2010, I'd stepped up the intention to find heart rocks in response to learning of my husband's cancer diagnosis. With surgery and treatment, he was likely to be fine, but still, the more heart rocks I could accumulate, the better I seemed to feel—thus the growing mountain on the shelf of his desk. I was great at finding these rocks. My eye had become adept at spotting them among the multitude of other shapes. There were teensy ones and hand-sized ones. They were from my walks in Pt. Reyes, north of San Francisco and along the American River near Sacramento. Some days I would come home with three or four, my pockets weighted down with hope. Other days I'd unfurl my palm and reveal just one precious stone I had held for the entire four miles.

Before I left on a visit to my hometown, my husband kissed me on the forehead and said gently, "Bring me back a heart rock." I let the kiss sink in and nodded. I planned to walk in the woods of my childhood; there were sure to be rocks waiting there.

On the day I reserved for my return to Little Sewickley Creek and the arched maples of Woodland Road, I felt nostalgic for the long days I had spent reading Annie Dillard in the woods by myself as a child. I parked by our old driveway and started my search for a nature-made token of my love. I knew how to do this; I thought it would be easy. *I will bring it home, a rock visitor from three thousand miles away, and carefully perch it with the other stone hope-keepers.*

The path was the same. I knew where it started—just before the ditch where my best friend and I found that filthy white cat almost dead, and where the jonquils first start their efforts after winter at the top of the curve in the road. Down I went, through ivy and fallen maple leaves, into the feeling of being small and solitary in the bigness of the woods and water. I wondered if anyone had been here in the years between now and when I had left. So many years—my life, our life, the kids, the future—the space of gentle emotional reflections opened for me.

At the creek bed, I began to scan the rocks. It requires a practiced gaze, one that doesn't get too locked into detail, and yet holds a specific awareness. My eyes were looking for the point of a heart, or the crevice that indicated the joining of two lobes. I let my mind wander, but my eyes stayed alert.

One time I tried to see if this method of finding heart shapes would work with other shapes or constructions. I changed my intention and looked for "elf booties." My eyes were then able to find the narrow calf shape and little toe bumps. Another time I wanted to notice only rocks that sported one white line encircling the circumference. I found both kinds. My shift in seeing worked, but I wasn't half as interested in miniature boots as I was in hearts.

At the creek, I passed under the covered bridge and navigated the ill-placed stone that always jutted out too far, the very stone that had caused me to fall off the frozen path into icy water one winter while trying to squeeze past. I felt myself get frustrated. There were no rocks to fill my pocket, nothing to warm with my fingers. I didn't want to go home empty handed.

So I crouched near the waterfall, hugged my knees, and took a breath. There were always heart rocks. Today wouldn't disappoint. The silty, smooth stones were all treasures. I watched them as I rested my chin on my knee.

Then I spied something among the muddy rocks. It was not a heart shape, but it did have a point. I reached into the wet sand and gasped as the spearhead I picked up fit perfectly into my hand. Each side had been flaked symmetrically to form a long narrow oval. It felt solid and sharp. I took a startled breath when I realized how very, very old it would have to be.

We used to find arrowheads in our garden every summer, but I had never found anything at the creek, and nothing like this 300-year-old artifact. *So this is the heart-stone I've been looking for?* I thought. My own heart beat faster when I realized that the spearhead had been down here all these years, accompanying me silently as I transitioned from one version of self to another, undiscovered until now.

That night, when I called my husband to check in, I told him, "I couldn't find a heart rock."

"That's okay," he reassured me. "I already have a heart rock mountain."

"But I found something totally amazing to add to the pile on your desk," I told him. "It's a surprise, and I know you will love it."

I carried the spearhead in my pocket for the rest of the visit and all the way home. When I placed my unexpected treasure in his palm, I silently vowed to keep looking—not just for heart rocks, but for all that I could see.

2

GETTING STARTED

Creative Process Assessment

Before we start looking at the five stages of the creative process in detail, it will be helpful to provide an experiential assessment of your relationship with each stage of the creative process. The following activity uses the creative process associated with the act of creating a drawing. I have chosen a drawing as our starting place because it is an accessible experience that you can do and reflect upon immediately. It is quite common for therapists to discover that the strengths and weakness associated with their art processes are directly related to their challenges and stuck places in their therapeutic work.

In starting this assessment, I suggest that you gather your supplies first, then read Step One. Do the art activity in Step One before you read Step Two. Then read Step Two and complete the art activity. As a final step, complete the questionnaire.

Step One

1. Gather your supplies:
   - two sheets of drawing paper (at least 8.5″ x 11″)
   - drawing tools: chalk pastels, oil pastels, or crayons
   - scissors
   - glue stick
   - writing paper or notebook.

2. On your first piece of paper, using one color of your drawing tool, make a quick scribble. You don't have to even look at the page—just scribble for about two seconds.

3. While looking at the piece of paper, generate at least three ideas about what you can turn your scribble into. This doesn't have to be a "something"—an abstract design or pattern is just fine. Rotate the paper a couple of times and see if the different perspective helps you come up with even more options. Make a list on a separate piece of paper.

4. Using **one** of the ideas that you came up with, add color, line, and texture to turn your scribble into something. Give yourself a good 15 minutes. Relax into it. See what happens. You can use as many colors as you like, and remember it doesn't have to be a "something."

Reflection

Write some thoughts down about how the process unfolded for you. Reflect on how it felt to scribble, generate ideas, choose an idea, and then actually draw.

Step Two

1. Now, find two parts of your drawing that you will cut out. Using your scissors (or just tearing it—who said there were absolute rules?), cut these two parts out of your first drawing.

2. Glue the two parts onto your second sheet of paper.

3. Now add lines and color in order to make these two "things" (from your first drawing) into something. Watch what happens: observe your thoughts, feelings, internal narration.

Reflection

Write some thoughts down about how the process unfolded for you. Reflect on how it felt to cut out pieces of your drawing, glue them down, come up with a new idea, and finally draw.

Questionnaire

Answer all of the following questions with a Yes or a No. Try to limit your responses to your experience of the art activity that you have just completed instead of trying to think about other creative activities or your work as a therapist. If you get curious, you can use this questionnaire for those other activities later.

Incubating

1. Finding time to start this art activity was difficult.
2. When I first looked at my scribble, I felt frustrated because I couldn't see anything to turn it into.
3. When I starting thinking of ideas for my scribble, I had too many; they were coming too fast.
4. I found myself thinking too far ahead and got stuck with comparing my drawing to others'.
5. I found myself worrying about how my drawing was going to turn out.
6. I noticed pressure on myself to make this project really good, not just okay.
7. I figured out what my scribble was going to be instantly and couldn't think of other options after that.
8. I think I rushed my ideas because I just wanted to get on with the drawing.
9. I noticed self-critical thoughts that hindered my ability to generate ideas.

Initial Idea

1. I had a difficult time choosing one idea from my list.
2. I wanted to be able choose the very best idea and couldn't identify which idea that was.
3. I overanalyzed the idea that I wanted to use.
4. I wondered if anyone would think my idea was too weird, or silly, or stupid, or _____ (fill in the blank with a negative adjective).
5. I took choosing an idea very seriously, maybe too seriously.

6. I needed to know that my idea was the right one for me.
7. I was afraid to choose an idea because I would then have to commit to it and in the end I might not like it.

Diving In

1. When I started to draw, I was tense or anxious.
2. When I started to draw, I felt pressure to perform or do it "right."
3. As I was drawing, I had critical thoughts about what my drawing looked like.
4. In order to even start drawing, I had to tell myself that my drawing didn't matter and it was just an exercise.
5. I spent a long time figuring out the first color that I was going to use in my drawing.
6. The scribbling was fine, but when it came to actually drawing I felt myself pulling away or losing interest.
7. I felt scared to start to draw because I didn't know if I could pull it off.
8. I was tempted to look up an image on the internet so that I could have a guide for how to do my drawing.

Flexible Commitment

1. I was drawing, but then I made a mistake and wanted to start all over again.
2. My drawing didn't end up being what I'd initially planned and that bugged me and made me want to stop or start over.
3. I liked my first drawing and I had a really hard time cutting it up to make the second drawing.
4. Once I cut out the pieces for Step Two, they didn't change and my second drawing was the same as my first.
5. I experienced a conflict, as though my drawings wanted to be one way and I wanted them to be another way.
6. The content of my drawing (either first or second) became too personal and I didn't want to keep going because I felt too vulnerable.

7. I was very frustrated with the directions and found myself wanting to do something different, but I didn't.
8. I kept wondering if I was doing it "right."

Note

Flow is not included in the questionnaire because it is impossible to get stuck or blocked while you are in this stage of your creative process. Flow is a wonderful stage and is the result of not getting blocked in the other four stages.

Scoring

Your YES answers indicate possible sources of being blocked. If you have three or more YES answers in one stage, it is likely that you have a pattern of getting blocked in this particular stage of your creative process.

In the following chapters, we will look closely at each stage, exploring how each stage feels and what we must do in order to prevent getting blocked or stuck. I will share stories that are designed to elucidate each stage of the creative process as it applies to the therapeutic process. I will also invite you to engage in art activities that can help you practice navigating each stage. While all of the stories and art invitations provide a rich backdrop for understanding the creative process, it could be especially helpful to concentrate on the art invitations associated with the particular stage(s) that your assessment identified as potential stuck places.

How to Define "Art"

You may consider art to be something that is made for its aesthetic value and should be exhibited in a gallery or hung in your home or office. Art is much more than that. For the purpose of further discussion and investigation in this book, I'd like to propose that we broaden the definition. Art comes in all shapes and sizes. Writing, dancing, singing, painting, and acting (to name a few) are common activities that result in the creation of art. But every creative endeavor—from delivering a speech to inventing new software—requires problem solving. When we problem solve, we utilize the creative process by generating options, making new connections, seeing from multiple perspectives, treating mistakes as opportunities, taking risks, and trying new things. I invite you to consider your clinical work and every other problem-solving endeavor as art. In this book, there are many art activities that will become your art. As such, I'd like to offer you some guidelines on how best to relate to your art.

Some Guidelines on Ways to Relate to Your Art

The art invitations in this book are designed to help you link theoretical concepts with individualized experience. They ask you to reach inside your inner world and make it visible. This isn't an easy thing to do. It takes courage, time, and tolerance for not-knowing. It requires a great deal of permission giving on your part: permission to explore, experiment, and be in a new experience. The act of taking a nonverbal, formerly unexpressed thought or feeling and making it into a visually externalized picture can be powerful and freeing.

I'd like to offer you some specific support around your art-making activities, which include ways to relate to your art so that you can benefit and, hopefully, even enjoy the experience.

Value Your Art

Do you value your art?

Do you treat it with the appreciation and loving kindness that it deserves?

Do you consider each and every creative endeavor, even the total flops, to be vital to your well-being?

When you were little, your mother or father might have proudly displayed your preschool finger painting on the refrigerator door. You might have had someone take pictures or videos of you dancing, singing, playing a musical instrument, or doing any number of artful activities. If you had a particularly enthusiastic grandmother, like I did, you would have had wall hangings and pillows hand-embroidered with your very own drawings used as the pattern. Sometimes the message is very, very clear: art is valued and encouraged, and the art maker is nurtured.

Much of the time the message is clear, but not in a positive way. It's possible you felt judged for your art—really good, really bad, better than, worse than. In these cases, unfortunately, your worthiness was correlated with the value (or lack thereof) that someone else placed on your art. It's very common to lose touch with the liberating excitement ushered in by any art-making endeavor as a result of this kind of experience. It is a reasonable decision, then, not to pursue creative expression. In these cases, folks tend to scratch art making off the list. You might have started to think of art making as a waste of time or something to avoid entirely because of the sure judgment and criticism it will bring.

What messages do you carry with you?
How do they impact your ability to dive into the art-making invitations set forth in this book?

Sometimes it takes a shift in perspective or a purposeful, mule-like determination to value your art. My friend Hannah Hunter repurposes only slightly exciting art quilts she has made into new and interesting collage inventions. She could just throw the "failures" out, but she knows that they will feed another creative endeavor someday, so she values them for what they are—potential beginnings. In her book *Bird by Bird* (1995), Anne Lamott treats her "shitty first drafts" as small children and with an endearing curiosity. She writes them down so they can have a "romp" around. She knows that the act of letting them out to play will lead to something, and rather than criticizing their rowdy havoc, she loves them into being. In 2006 I attended a Rodin exhibit at the Legion of Honor in San Francisco. The exhibited included the tiny clay maquettes that Rodin kept for inspiration. They were rough little nothings, but his fingers obviously craved forming these doodly shapes. He let it happen and valued them enough to keep them around. The Legion of Honor valued them, too, and included them in his retrospective as vital pieces of information about his grander-scale creative endeavors.

So whether you love or hate the artwork that you make, please value it. Treat it the same way you would treat a preschooler's finger painting. Let it represent an important expression for you and consider putting it up on your refrigerator. Your creative process will benefit.

Slather on Compassion

I truly believe you deserve as much compassion for your own undertakings as you would bestow on another. If you would put your toddler's scribble on the fridge, try allowing that same sense of celebration for your scribbles (no matter in what form they come). If you would excuse—or perhaps not even notice—mistakes in someone else's concerted effort to create, then please feel free to excuse your own.

Soften Expectations

Creativity is stifled by expectations. If you expect that your first draft will be elegant or your third painting will land you a spot in a gallery show or your e-course will go viral or your success with a client will make you a great therapist, you are going to kill your creativity. Instead, ask yourself these four questions:

1. Did I experiment?
2. Did I engage?
3. Did I stay curious?
4. Did I take a risk at some point along the way?

When you can answer yes to these questions, you are valuing your art and giving yourself permission to really engage in your creative process.

Celebrate Everything

When you celebrate, you send yourself the message that your creative endeavors matter. Small creative successes add up to creativity confidence. When you feel confident, you can Dive In and make art without the filter of fear holding you back. Yes, you might make a mistake, but even that could lead to something remarkable. A sketchbook or journal is a good way for you to keep track of your creative efforts. Make notes, take pictures, comment, record, express excitement, and cultivate gratitude for your commitment to be creative.

Share with Others

Think of someone safe with whom you could share your art activities. Not just the good-looking creative moments—even the disasters that helped you get to the next new, amazing, creative step. Every time you share, you invite others into your creative process and inspire them to be more creative as well. (Please read the Appendix to get more inspiration about forming a group.)

Find Your Inner Art Patron, Quiet Your Inner Critic

In order to sustain your creativity, you need a way to quiet your inner critic. The most successful form of support comes from a relationship with your inner art patron. Throughout history, art patrons have supported artists by inviting them to live in their homes and castles, commissioning their work, and paying for their living expenses and art supplies. If not for art patronage, many of the brilliant masters' works would not exist. Michelangelo was supported by Julius II while he painted the Sistine Chapel (Condivi, 2007). Ludovico Sforza was Leonardo da Vinci's patron for 17 years (Boston Museum of Science, n.d.). Ambroise Voullard abandoned his law career in 1895 to buy 150 paintings by Cezanne (who was virtually unknown) and exhibit them in Paris in the artist's first-ever show (Art Institute of Chicago, 2007).

A patron has a unique relationship to an artist's art. When a patron enters into a supportive relationship with an artist, it means the patron believes in and admires the artist. A patron sees potential but, more than that, he values what the artist is saying and doing in present time. Voullard could barely afford to buy all of Cezanne's paintings. He didn't even have the money to frame them all for an exhibit. Nevertheless, he found an old farmhouse where the paintings hung for Cezanne's first show. The patron's job is to support the artist's continued creative endeavors. The patron does not need to supply critiques or evaluation for the artist. The public and other artists do plenty of that. Rather, the patron's support serves to help the artist continue to create despite criticism or judgment. It's a powerful relationship for both artist and patron.

Most of us don't have the fortune of knowing a Voullard or Julius II. However, every one of us has an internal patron. Just like an inner child who remembers for us how to play, our internal patron supports our art. If we consider therapy our art form, we can celebrate our ability to navigate the emotional canvas like nobody's business. We know when to slow our brush strokes of conversation and when to lean into our sculpting tools to make a deeper impression. We are stunning in our art-making endeavors. And our patron has every bit as much to do with this as our artist does.

> *Does your patron believe in your art abilities and see even more poten-*
>   *tial for you?*
> *Does your patron help to sustain your ability to show up every day?*
> *Has your patron invested in your training because you are worth it?*
> *Does your patron know that you will need that little nap mid-afternoon*
>   *and make sure that you schedule it in?*

In addition to all of these supportive things, your inner art patron can quiet your inner critic. It can be a voice of encouragement that helps counter the negative judgments that come from the critical part of you that is often called the inner critic. Because your patron has already invested in your art and already believes in your abilities, he or she has automatic rebuttals to many of the mean things your inner critic will say. Unlike your inner critic, who loves to capitalize on mistakes, your inner art patron understands that there will be ups and downs, mistakes and successes.

When you get to know your patron better and really nurture that relationship that already exists inside, your patron can act as a buffer or mediator and shield you from the critic. Here's a story about a real-life example.

In 2002, I had the privilege of being hired by Jack Goswick to work as an art therapist for a juvenile sex offender treatment program. The ultimate art patron, he gave me a perfect studio space, a healthy budget for supplies, and free rein to create an art therapy program that complemented his residential program. I was in heaven. I felt supported, liberated, inspired. He didn't micromanage, but he was there when I needed to talk through my ideas.

I decided that I wanted to build a darkroom and teach a therapeutic photography class. Jack was enthusiastic and intrigued. He presented the new plan at a staff meeting. Some of the staff were supportive, but a few were highly critical. They shot down the idea with worst-case scenarios about a bunch of juvenile sex offenders being in the dark together. They questioned the therapeutic benefit and my ability to create a classroom environment. While Jack heard all of these responses calmly, I could barely sit still in my seat. I wanted to bolt out of the classroom and never come back to work. He said to his staff, "We're going to let her try, and I'm going to support her in any way I can. Some of your concerns are valid, but they are not constructive. If you'd like to give suggestions that would help her implement this group, set up a meeting. If not, direct your complaints to me."

There was a meeting. Several of the teachers and therapists joined me. We strategized a safety plan. We made a list of criteria that students had to meet before being admitted into the group. We made sure there were therapeutic objectives for the class that matched students' individual therapy objectives. And

I got to make a darkroom and teach my therapeutic photography course for two years.

I couldn't have persevered without my art patron Jack's support and mediation. In that meeting, I wasn't in a position to argue with the critics. I couldn't defend myself in such a hurt state. I felt bullied and shut down. All I wanted to do was run. Jack was the one who stepped in and talked to my critics. He acted as my patron and remained supportive of my art even in the face of judgment. He, not I, had the power to hold the space, and he did so without waffling.

You see, if you let your art patron handle talking to your inner critic, you have a better chance. So does your art.

How can you do this internally?
How about getting really clear on what your inner art patron would say in a situation like mine?

Write a script, imagine a play, get into the dialogue. If you ask your inner art patron to do the talking, it gives you a break. It lets you continue with your art and bask in your patron's support.

Emphasize Process over Product

When you respond to an art invitation that asks you to create something, it is very easy to emphasize your end product. You begin making art in order to accomplish the end goal. This can be a very good thing for your art in that it gives you something to work toward, a concept to think about as you embark on your creative endeavor.

However, if you only focus on the end product, you are likely to devalue the process and miss out on the rich experience of your art making. It can also set you up for re-encountering some negative messaging about the worthiness of your art making in general.

Instead, consider treating the art invitations as entry points. They are simply invitations that are meant to inspire your process. If your completed art does not end up being a watch

(Chapter 4) or rainbow (Chapter 3), for example, that is not at all a bad thing. You can't do it wrong.

When you allow your creative process to guide your art making, it will take all kinds of unexpected turns. The richness lies in your experience of art making, not in the end product.

Here are some guidelines that can help remind you to emphasize the process over the product.

1. *Don't* be concerned with the meaning behind your artwork. While you are in the process of making your art, it's too early to understand the meaning. Delay any kind of interpretation as much as possible. Tell yourself, "My art will change and develop as I go. I can't pin down anything about my art while I'm still in the process of creating."

2. *Do* think or talk about your artwork without searching for meaning. Instead of interpreting, you can narrate your process. While you are working, think to yourself, "I'm using big brush strokes of red. Now I'm adding blue circles. The border is becoming yellow." If you are sharing with others, you can talk about the steps you took in your art making and narrate the process that way. This is a beautifully validating way to attend to your process. The more you focus on the here-and-now of your art making, the less you focus on the product and interpretation.

3. *Celebrate* your "I don't knows." If you find yourself not knowing where to start or how to keep going once you've started, remind yourself that this is a crucial part of your creative process. You are probably Diving In (Chapter 5) or needing to exercise Flexible Commitment (Chapter 6). Rather than doubting your product, take yourself back to your process and celebrate that you are, in fact, right where you need to be. When you don't know, new discoveries happen. Instead of thinking about product, ask yourself, "What's the next color that looks good to me?" Then, "How does that next color want to show up on the page?"

4. *Ask* "How was that for me?" Once you've completed your art invitation, don't leap right away into evaluating the product. First, reflect on the process. Ask yourself, "How did that feel to make?" "What about it was easy or hard?" "What stages of the creative process happened for me, and how did they go?"

Once you've honored your art-making process, you are more primed to think about the meaning or message that your art might provide. Then, and only then, invite yourself and others (if you are working in a group) to share on that level.

Summary

The Creative Process Assessment assisted in identifying initial strengths and weaknesses in the way you navigate your creative process. We have considered important factors that go into valuing your art. Now we are equipped to unpack each of the five stages of creativity. In the chapters that follow, we will look at what is required in order to navigate each stage specifically. The stories, case studies, and vignettes offer multiple contexts through which to see the creative process as it relates to therapy and art making. Each chapter is concluded by a set of questions to ponder and art invitations to do. Enjoy!

Part II

THE FIVE STAGES OF THE CREATIVE PROCESS

3

INCUBATING

All creative endeavors begin with a period of Incubation. This first stage is a crucial part of the creative process, and yet many of us try to skip over this pre-art/pre-session period because of the fast-paced, information-filled state of our lives. If an artist arrives in the studio with an intention to paint without having spent time in the Incubating stage, she stands frozen in front of her canvas, unable to make the first mark. If a writer shows up to her computer to begin the story without having allowed time for words to percolate, she feels disoriented and can't even begin one sentence. If a therapist begins a session without having allowed some Incubation time where she has let her thinking about her client be nimble and open to new ideas, the session can feel stagnant and repetitive, and she and her client may have the sense that nothing new is happening.

For a therapist, Incubation is beautifully permissive. It is the act of allowing our thoughts to soften and take a vacation from analyzing our clients' issues. While Incubating can feel challenging to our typical way of working because it asks us to lower our boundaries and allow ourselves to think about clients outside of session, it can also help us usher in more creative thoughts by offering an alternative to worrying.

Incubating is a soft way of thinking. To soften our thoughts, we need to trust that ideas come from many different sources, and that the pressure we tend to put on ourselves to come up with the right idea or plan is unnecessary. A declaration of trust in this kind of soft thinking, otherwise known as divergent thinking, is commonly heard when someone can't remember the name of a movie or a restaurant. They will say, "I'm sure it will come to mind in a minute or right before I fall asleep tonight." The act of allowing our brains to wrestle with the puzzle in the background, without our having to focus directly on it, is a softening in our thinking. And, sure enough, without focusing directly on the forgotten name, there will be a moment of remembering, or a reminder that pops out of nowhere, and the thought is retrieved.

Incubating can be a bit disorienting at first because it taps into such a broad range of thought and experience. It is very different from the analytical act of reviewing our technique or theoretical approach or the latest literature on our client's presenting issue because it utilizes much more. Our life experiences, our hobbies, and our interests all contribute and get woven into our art and our creative process. Once we become practiced in Incubating, we come to value our brain's ability to come up with extraordinarily valuable ideas that we hadn't been able to access without Incubating. These ideas become seeds for the next step of the creative process, the Initial Idea, and set the stage for inspired and effective therapy sessions.

The Wind-Up Doll

Donna had been a therapist for 25 years. She had a high success rate in helping female clients resolve their early childhood trauma, and she was in great demand in her community. While she was grateful for her success, she felt tired and stuck in her work. She described herself as a wind-up doll repeating the same mini-lectures to her clients session after session. She had tried to come up with new ideas or unique ways of approaching client issues, but she felt stunted and chronically uninspired. She worried that one day she would wake up and be unable to get herself to work. She feared that the rut would get so deep, it would become unbearable, and she would have no choice but to retire despite her lifelong dedication to helping.

Donna didn't think of herself as a creative person, but she had recently gone to a weekend collage class that she enjoyed immensely. Her experience there had sparked her curiosity. She had connected with a playful, imaginative part of herself in the class. In particular, she had been tickled by the realization that making a collage about her role as a therapist invited her to think so differently about the subject. In her collage, she had chosen two images: a woman reading in a hammock and a larger-than-life portrait of a man staring straight into the viewer's eyes. The juxtaposition of these two inspired her to see her role as a therapist differently. She tended to see herself as a supporter of her clients. Her hammock image emphasized the sense of relaxation and peace that she wanted to impart to them. But the man's intense gaze leaping out from the collage symbolized a part of her role as therapist that she had been missing. To her, this image represented challenge, excitement, and forging into the unknown with her clients. As a result of this collage experience, she began to wonder how she could show up in this intense and engaged way in her life and work. She wanted to learn new things and feel more creative, but she couldn't quite bring herself to do more collage on her own.

That is how Donna came to join my therapists' art group. In this group, therapists practice their creative process by using art materials in order to assist them in being more creative in their therapeutic process. For Donna, this was a perfect match. She was craving more creativity in all aspects of her life but she didn't know how to even begin to navigate her creative process. In the group, she expressed amazement at others' art processes. "How did you even think of that idea?" she would exclaim. She continued to feel stunted in her creativity. "I just don't think creatively," she said. "I'm stuck here, just like I'm stuck in my work with clients." Many days in group, she wouldn't get started with her art making until it was already too late to begin. Other days she would work quickly on an idea only to decide it was all wrong and throw it away.

Donna was having difficulty in the first stage of the creative process. Her ability to tolerate the fuzzy thinking that Incubation requires was limited. She liked to *know*, and she liked to be sure that her idea was a good one. In therapy, this meant that she relied on old stories and a repetitive approach with clients. In art, her ideas ran dry. Because she couldn't allow herself to let go and think divergently, she ended up obsessing about others' artwork in the group. She would wait too long and then, because it was too late, she would miss out on fulfilling her wish to be more imaginative and original.

Donna struggled with the fear that she wouldn't come up with anything worthwhile in her creative endeavors. Her doubt created resistance to even trying the art activity. She had such high expectations of herself as a therapist and as an artist that she cut herself off even before getting started.

In teaching Donna more about what it means to Incubate, one of the first skills I shared with her was brainstorming. Rather than criticizing or comparing herself to others, I asked her and the group to devote ten minutes to brainstorming before beginning an art activity. I would explain the art invitation for that day, and then we would go around the circle and generate endless options for responding to the art invitation. No option was stupid or bad. Everyone had to contribute. During these brainstorming sessions, Donna would become silly and playful and sometimes put her hand over her mouth in response to some of the ridiculous suggestions she would think of. In response to an art invitation to represent the experience of becoming fully present with a client, the ideas started out with doorway and threshold themes. Eventually the ideas expanded to more abstract and tangential ideas: "A mask over a heart." "A firefly in a jar." "A prism that fills your spine." "A mouse nest in a farmhouse." "Purple swirls inside a glass ball." The group brainstorming provided a stream of ideas that ranged from brilliant to illogical, thought provoking to downright absurd.

In this brainstorm practice, Donna learned that she could bring a different part of herself, a silly, playful part, to her Incubating. She learned that she couldn't force ideas to happen or wish them into existence—she had to allow them. She started to embrace her imagination with enthusiastic patience and allow her process more trust. She learned to replace her tendency to criticize and shut down her creative process with a brainstorming session. She started to rely on brainstorming as a way of softening her thinking and inviting new ideas.

This brainstorming practice also taught Donna the difference between Incubation and Procrastination. She recognized that the rut she experienced in doing therapy had to do with the same stuckness she felt in trying to start her art. In therapy, she would just rely on the same old thing rather than using her creativity to come up with uniquely specific interventions for her clients because she didn't use her thinking time in a creative way. She was actually Procrastinating rather than Incubating. She learned to tell the difference in emotional tone between the two. She recognized Incubation as hopeful, curious, pregnant with possibility, and Procrastination as lethargic, avoidant, heavy with dread. I asked her to remind herself that Incubation is part of the process, while Procrastination just stops the process.

Because Donna learned that her procrastination fed on inaction and judgment, whenever she felt its presence, she knew what she needed to do: she needed to brainstorm in that same loving, compassionate, and playful way that she had done with the group. She practiced this in her art-making activities and she also applied it to her sessions with clients.

As a result, Donna no longer stopped herself from being creative. She used playful brainstorming as a way to prevent procrastination and spawn new ideas. She felt better about herself and her creativity. She had the beginning piece of her creative process in place and was prepared to embrace the next stages with delight and enthusiasm. The mini-lectures that she used to tell in sessions started to change because she pulled in unique and interesting examples that applied specifically to her clients. Most importantly, she no longer dreaded sessions because she knew how to generate new ideas that were inspiring for both her clients and herself.

The Importance of Incubating

The expectations that we put on ourselves as therapists can be strangulating. We are smart and accustomed to sorting through facts. We really want to get it right. But, in our endeavor to analyze and glean insights, we paralyze our creativity. We end up stilted in our approach, and like Donna, we can feel uninspired and bored. Incubating sets the stage for our creativity. The rest of this chapter offers suggestions for how to shift expectations of therapy from "figuring out the right thing" to "Incubating as the first part of a creative therapeutic approach."

What Incubating Requires

- Cross-pollinating
- Breadth of learning
- Finding stillness.

Cross-Pollinating

If we don't want to be wind-up doll therapists like Donna was, we cannot simply copy and paste technique or blindly follow a step-by-step therapeutic protocol. We have to learn to cross-pollinate like Donna did. She used her collage work to discover a new approach to her clinical work, and learned to draw from her life experiences to enrich her mini-lectures and turn them into unique stories to help her clients. The idea that cross-pollinating is an important part of Incubating is exemplified in the quote: "Good artists copy, great artists steal," which has been attributed to various artists including Stravinsky and Picasso. When artists are inspired by existing ideas and inventions, they are, in essence, "stealing" an idea. Rather than copying, artists build upon an existing idea by rearranging or reorganizing it into something brand new. Picasso did this brilliantly when he "stole" Cubist ideas and applied them to his fascination with the human body and face to paint portraits like they had never been painted before.

Cross-pollinating can happen in many different situations. For example, we can be at a movie or watching TV when something suddenly makes us think of a specific client. Or we can be doing a favorite activity such as gardening and find ourselves relating the metaphor of weeding (for example) to a client's presenting issue.

Here's the catch. In order to benefit from cross-pollinating, we have to be open to thinking about clients outside of session. If we have too strong a boundary, the "leave the client at the office" approach, our out-of-session experiences will not connect to our work. It is often a relief for therapists to understand that thinking about clients outside of session is a natural creative process, and that we can embrace these thoughts as part of our Incubating stage. However, it is very important to differentiate between Incubating and worrying. If we worry about our clients outside of session, our thoughts are circular, obsessive, and disruptive. If we are Incubating, our thoughts are more open, free flowing, and diverse.

Donna learned to appreciate her love of cooking as a crucial element in her Incubating stage. Her cooking is a great example of cross-pollinating. She loved to improve on recipes by adding unique ingredients and took to naming the muffin recipes after her clients because she would end up thinking of them while trying new flavor combinations. She often brought her muffins and spreads to group for us to try. One of my favorite examples was the time she made corn muffins that contained a center of whole kernels. She had been thinking about the texture surprise that the muffin could deliver, and named it after a client who she realized had "a whole treasure trove of undigested sweetness." She used this idea to approach her client's anger issues from an entirely different direction the next time she met with him. Needless to say, the group thoroughly enjoyed the new muffin, "Larry's Surprise."

These seemingly spontaneous connections between unrelated concepts are exciting. They fuel the creative process with original thought. Often, cross-pollinating can lead us straight into the next stage of the creative process. This is when the Initial Idea comes automatically as an "aha" moment and marks the second stage, discussed in Chapter 4.

Breadth of Learning

There are also dry times when ideas don't seem to come and Incubating feels fruitless. In order to keep Incubation from grinding to an intolerable halt when this happens, we can make sure that we pursue multiple interests. To broaden our range of reading beyond therapy journals is to embrace a breadth of learning. When we value varied life experiences and hobbies that require different skill sets from the ones we use in our work, we shift our frame of reference in interesting ways. As Carl Rogers famously said about the training of therapists, "I'd rather have someone who read widely and deeply in literature or in physics, than to have someone who has always majored in psychology. I think that breadth of learning along with breadth of life experience are essential to becoming a good therapist" (Baldwin, 1987: p. 37).

I have watched many therapists add to their pool of knowledge in exciting ways. Many take up an exercise program such as yoga, running, or CrossFit that teaches them things about being in their bodies and meeting challenges. Others study interesting periods of history, plant a garden, or take improv classes. Holly, another therapist from my group, decided to finally take the singing lessons that she had never made time for in the past. Her experience of being a beginner at something gave her renewed compassion. She was thrilled at her ability to overcome perform-ance anxiety at her holiday recital and felt she had tapped into an entirely new frame of reference for her anxious clients.

Finding Stillness

Stillness is a momentary reprieve from the incessant analysis of our work. It is the meditative act of getting our mind to stop the ongoing narrative and the endless internal dialogues. It is allowing ourselves to *not* think, and to instead just be.

Part of the creative process is to allow what needs to come by sitting in stillness. But achieving stillness in a world of busyness is difficult because of the pull to continue doing, moving, acting. Our to-do lists can be seductive—one more client, a few more phone calls, fit in this errand. If we don't stop to notice, we become lost in the whirl. But when we let things settle, the reward is astonishing. When we access calm, we can self-reflect and capture moments and connections that might have just skipped by.

In any given day or moment, you can invite yourself to seek the delicious languor of stillness. The ongoing commitment to welcome this hush into a day is the start of a creative life. Without stillness, there can be no self-reflection, no new connections, no inspiration. I like to think of the visceral soothing that comes from being at the ocean or watching a swollen river flow. When we stand there, so tiny and open, the watery forces show us that we are also still. The tides pull and the waves crash, and there we are on the shore, with our one heartbeat and our still limbs and our swirling puzzle pieces being invited to fit into the bigger scheme of things.

My morning walks are times of stillness. I make them strenuous and long. And at some point on the trail, I always stop to watch for eddies on the river or herons in the trees. These are times when my movement slows and the rhythm of my walking stalls to a quiet dreaminess. I can feel my thoughts sort themselves and find solid places to settle. Inevitably, I walk out of the woods with a heart full of newness and inspiration. Words, phrases, ahas are all sparks for the creative beginnings that I will develop during the course of my day.

When the therapists who attend my workshops first start planning for stillness or self-reflection, they say that it feels as if they are trying to will themselves to meditate but their minds refuse to participate. If our schedules are full and activities compete for attention, this is understandable. In order to achieve a sense of stillness, we may need to find something that allows our hands or feet to do something. I often recommend that my workshop participants use rhythmic movement to help free them up and tell their body they are up to something good. Walking in nature is certainly a great activity. Doing handwork (knitting, embroidery, crochet) is another.

When we give our senses something to invest in, we involve parts of our being that don't often get used. If we have a piece of colorful felt, some shiny beads, and the sense of a swirling line, the feeling of sinking in becomes accessible. When we walk in nature and feel the cool air on our skin and listen to the rhythm of our shoes on the earth, the feeling of open stillness arrives. When our hands work with something or our bodies engage, our thoughts can wander and eventually weave. The experience of stillness wraps around us.

Rituals

Rituals can assist us in cultivating stillness when it feels hard to come by in our ordinary modes of being. Artists often have idiosyncratic rituals on which they rely in order to successfully Incubate. Novelist Isabelle Allende will only begin a new writing project on January 1, which allows her many months of Incubation time. Writer Toni Morrison does her Incubation while driving to work or mowing the lawn. She fits in this time between teaching and parenting, and intentionally forgoes activities such as cocktail parties that would distract her from this "brooding" time. Dancer and choreographer Twyla Tharp (2003) teaches her students to Incubate by bringing a stool up to the front of class and asking them to think of 60 different uses for it. The first 10 or 20 ideas are easy and predictable, but after that, their ideas become more unique. Once they have limbered their brains with this activity, the students are primed for the second stage of the creative process, the Initial Idea.

Whatever the ritual, artists understand that Incubating time comes when their mind is relaxed and not overly focused on the solution to the creative challenge. I have a therapist friend who relies on her evening baths as her Incubating ritual. She relaxes in the tub after work and washes away her experiences with clients from that day. Then she allows her mind to wander and gently open to the next day's schedule of clients. When I start my morning walk with a specific client in mind, without having to think any further about the client during the walk, an idea will pop out of the trees for me and I will feel inspired for the next session.

Whatever the activity or ritual, we have to have respect for this stage of the creative process. It takes patience. It takes trust. It also takes commitment. When we learn to work with this first stage, we are setting ourselves up to have brilliant bolts of inspiration that will energize our creative processes over and over again.

Procrastination is Not Incubation

When we recognize that Incubation requires time, it is easy to start to confuse Procrastination with Incubation. Both require time. It is not uncommon to be overcome by the urge to clean the bathroom or art studio before starting a creative endeavor. Research tangents, phone calls that become urgent, and elaborate dinner recipes can all be examples of either Procrastination or Incubation. As Donna learned in this chapter's opening vignette, it is important to know the difference. The following story helps explain the difference between Procrastination and Incubation.

A couple of years ago, I found two goose eggs in the same week on my daily walks at the river. I found the first one on Monday. I knew it was abandoned because none of the squawking sentinels at the pond beat their wings aggressively when I reached down to rescue the egg from its poor excuse of a nest on top of the sand. It was big and beautiful. For the rest of my walk, I began to hatch plans to borrow a friend's Dremel tool and cut the egg into concentric ovals and use them as frames like I had seen at a recent craft fair. But when I got home, my daughter and husband had different plans for the egg. Into their makeshift incubator it went.

On Tuesday, I found another abandoned goose egg. Once again, no dog-sized bird came rushing to claim it. I found this one at the water's edge—too cold for any sweet pre-baby to be happy. Just the same, into the incubator it went.

For me, Monday's egg represented Incubation. Tuesday's egg represented Procrastination. Same object, same symbol, probably same goose mama—yet I had a totally different relationship with each. When I picked up Monday, I felt a sense of wonder and hope. My daughter told me that there was an ever-expanding dark spot that she could see when she shone a flashlight on the egg. I felt giddy with anticipation. I conjured images of a tiny goose beak poking out of its newly broken egg. I was content with waiting because the overwhelming feeling was positive. Either way, whether Monday turned into a goose or an art project, I felt this time of Incubating had been valuable.

In contrast, when I picked up Tuesday, I felt dread and heaviness. My daughter said that there was no dark spot that she could see with her flashlight, but she reminded me that this had been true with Monday for a little while too. She remained hopeful, but I didn't have good images for Tuesday. Mostly my thoughts involved how badly Tuesday would smell if I ever decided to use that Dremel tool to make the oval frame art project.

The difference in my relationship with Monday and Tuesday, Incubation and Procrastination, had to do with the emotional tone. Like Donna, I recognized that Incubation was hopeful, curious, and pregnant with possibility, while Procrastination was lethargic, avoidant, and heavy with dread.

To recognize the difference between Incubation and Procrastination is one key to beginning any creative endeavor. It is crucial to be able to identify when we are hanging out waiting for things to hatch (Incubation) and when we are pretending to hang out and wait, but are actually avoiding something or creating resistance (Procrastination).

When we apply this to the art of doing therapy, I like to use worry as a gauge. The presence of our worry alone is not a good gauge; we all worry about our clients on occasion. But the presence of worry to the extent that it becomes a sleep-interrupting preoccupation or an idea-stifling pall over our creativity is a very good gauge. If we think about a client and notice that worry is an overshadowing part of our relationship, we are Procrastinating. This also means that we are not being creative. We are blocked, stuck, destined to go round and round in our thoughts with nothing new coming in.

If, on the other hand, our worry gauge is at small or unnoticeable levels when we think about a client, we are probably Incubating. If we feel curious and willing to hang out long enough to witness an outcome or see the next step, we are definitely Incubating.

How to Get Better at Incubating

Incubating isn't a one-size-fits-all activity. It looks different for each of us. Donna found that she needed to shift her thoughts and allow brainstorming time. Holly now relies on her singing lessons. Toni Morrison and many other artists have to integrate their Incubation time into the obligations of their busy lives. It is a mistake to automatically assume that our Incubation requires long, uninterrupted hours of isolation and dreaminess. As with every part of the creative process, there is no one right way to Incubate. Whatever formula works for us, we have to embrace it and apply it. The stories that follow illustrate the paths others have found to Incubating.

Collect Riffs

In the 1980s, Richard Elliot was an up-and-coming sax player with a well-earned spot in the funky horn section of the urban soul band Tower of Power. Because I had a huge crush on Richard, I followed the band all around Northern California. It was fun to try to get him to hang out after the shows, but the best part was the lesson he taught me at the Concord Jazz Festival in 1987.

The sun was hot and the open-air stadium was loud. The Tower of Power had delivered a funky groove that boosted the effects of the vodka and orange juice my friends and I had snuck into the festival. And I was extra giddy because, in my naive enthusiasm, I had convinced Richard to come hang out with us after his performance.

Richard Elliot came sauntering up, squeezed onto the bench beside little ol' just-out-of-college me, and took a sip from my jug. Silently I swooned. I don't remember which bands we heard or how long we were there, but I do remember not knowing what to say. He was listening to the music intently, and questions like, "Where were you born? How many siblings to you have?" seemed ridiculous. So I just sat and listened intently with him.

But I'm a talker, and eventually the lack of words was killing me. So I asked him, "What are you listening for?"

He turned away from the stage and looked directly at me. "Riffs," he said. "I'm listening for interesting riffs. They inspire me."

I became curious. "What do you do with a riff that inspires you?"

Richard said, "I draw a small line that depicts the riff in my head—the up and down and round and round of the music—and then, eventually, I try it out in my own music. It's like a new vocabulary word—it enriches what I have to say."

We spent the rest of the afternoon listening together. Every time one of us would hear an inspiring riff, we would nudge the other's shoulder and nod slightly in recognition.

To this day, I collect "riffs." I hear them at conferences, on TV, and from clients. I read them in novels, newspapers, blogs, and tweets. The little riffs become new vocabulary for whatever it is I have to say.

Here are some of my recent favorites:

From a client: "It should be a law that we all spend eighteen
minutes a day in nature."
From a conference: "What is your dose of buoyancy for clients?"
From a training course: "Don't look to thoughts to do more for
you than they can."
From a workshop participant: "Creativity is treating the Unknown
as an ally, not an enemy."

The smallest phrase can be a riff that spurs us on and breathes
new life into our next "gig." Richard Elliot would invite us to collect them, make art with them, and weave them into our vocabulary. I even love to think about using them in session with a client.

Shift Focus

When I was little, our next-door neighbor Al was a puzzle nut.
He always had a jigsaw puzzle in progress covering the fold-out
card table that inhabited the middle of his living room. I was
impatient with those meticulous kinds of activity but would
occasionally pass by Al's house on my bicycle route to the park.
He'd be outside pruning his roses or holding a garden hose,
seemingly entranced by his fern watering. I would call out
to him, "Hiya, Al, watcha doin'?" He'd smile and wave: "Just
working on my latest puzzle." And sure enough, many times
when my Nana went over to visit, I'd tag along and marvel at
the neatly fitted accomplishment of a puzzle, complete on the
card table.

But I didn't understood how Al's gardening fit into his work
as a puzzle master. He obviously knew a secret, one that I have
only recently come to understand because of my own endeavors to master puzzling.

Al's secret? Sometimes we just have to shift our focus in order
to allow our creative process to do its magic.

I can't tell you how often I have the sensation of an idea or
a solution just about to arrive, landing gear out, ready to glide

gently onto the perfect spot in my brain. I can feel the soft ease of understanding, the spark of an aha, the jumping-up-and-down excitement that it's finally landed and ready.

I think this happens in our work as healing professionals. It doesn't happen in every session, but sometimes there's that lingering feeling that something is about to open up and show itself—some insight that could be so helpful it would rock our client's world. Usually it comes from that mishmash state of seemingly unrelated parts that our questions and interactions have led us to. We see the many different patterns and emotional dynamics that clients bring to our offices. We've gathered the puzzle pieces on the card table and now have to put them together into a cohesive image.

When that sensation is lingering, I've learned, just like Al, to get the heck out of the way—to go out and smell the roses, listen to the birds, talk to a loved one. Sure enough, when I stop forcing it all to fit, that sweet puzzle piece floats right into position. The times when I come back and share the idea with a client and he or she feels that same relief of having found the missing puzzle piece, we get to celebrate that special moment together. And I secretly thank Al for showing me the value of shifting focus in order to get there.

No One "Right" Way

Carla's life was a mad rush. She was a busy therapist with a full-time private practice, three active kids under ten, and a traveling husband. Most days felt like a juggling act that she could barely get through, and she felt her creativity was really suffering.

When we first met at my online workshop, Carla expressed her desperation for the feeling of spacious creative expression. She was envious of people in the course who could spend days completing their art assignments. Her finished art was always the last to be shared in the Facebook group. Inevitably she posted an image with an apology for not getting it done sooner.

Carla felt the same sense of inadequacy about her meetings with clients that she did about the completion of her art assignments. Lack of time and the pull of her other responsibilities seemed to take her away from that quiet space of thinking about her clients that she craved. Her constant rush was frustrating and she often went around with the sense that she was moving way too fast.

I adored Carla's intensity and sensed that her presence with clients was powerful. I imagined her sitting down in her office, the blur of speed that she'd trailed behind her getting vacuumed back into her body within a split second.

Carla didn't doubt her ability to be present and engaged with clients. She called the space she inhabited with them "sacred." She loved her work; it was a reprieve from the noise of her life, which she saw as getting in the way.

During one of our sessions, I asked her to try on the idea that her entire juggling act of life was an act of Incubating. I asked her to stop compartmentalizing her art and her life and to see them as an integrated way of being. Her work with clients and her kids' bedtime routine, for instance, could both be creative acts. She didn't have to wait to think of herself as creative until she was able to carve out the time she imagined necessary to think about her clients.

Carla softened with this new way of seeing her hectic schedule. She started to understand that there were experiences outside of session that were valuable to her sessions, and vice versa. She could imagine her life being held in a bigger frame rather than multiple boxes stacked up haphazardly. But she still criticized herself and compared herself to others in the group who seemed to take more time to consider things, to create, and to reflect.

I had Carla start an "Incubating Journal." I wanted her to begin to take note of the ideas that came flooding into her once she arrived in her seat as a therapist. I asked her to become aware that this was happening rather than leaving it as a preverbal experience.

Carla began recording memos to herself and her phone began to fill with ideas. She would copy some of the ideas down and email them to me. The exclamation points in her emails were exciting. Carla was understanding that her Incubation did not require spacious quiet time. By capturing her ideas in that split second of catching up with herself, she was practicing her unique style of Incubating. She was tickled to learn that she'd been thinking about her clients without actually being conscious of thinking, and the ideas that she generated were powerful and meaningful.

Carla was able to understand that her style of Incubation didn't fit her initial expectations and, as a result, was able to stop apologizing for her "lateness." She knew she had to come right up against a deadline in order for the idea to pop. She had a new trust in her creative process, and, as a result, could hold the rest of her hectic life in higher regard. Yes, it was tiring, and she often wanted a rest. But she also embraced her creative style more fully and was happier and more freely creative than she had ever been.

Incubating with Clients

In addition to trusting and allowing Incubation to occur outside of session, we can also apply the same ideas during a session with a client. When we utilize divergent thinking and brainstorming while meeting with a client, we are intentionally merging the creative process with the therapeutic process. When we share some of the thoughts and invite our clients to contribute, we enter into a collaborative Incubation stage. In this sense, we are continually partnering with our own creativity and teaching our clients to do the same.

Pulling the Taffy

"You ask such strange and good questions!" exclaimed Toby, who had just completed an abstract self-portrait using scraps of colored paper and yarn. It was our third session, and prior to her beginning her art activity, we had gone through a round of Incubating together. Toby was an interior designer who looked every bit as put together as the upscale professional offices she regularly decorated. Her eye for color and scale were evident in her jewel-toned blouses and one-of-a-kind matching necklaces. She was stunning to look at, but her appearance hadn't masked her lonely eyes. She had come to work with me to find her way back to a happier time when she had been less constricted by her social anxiety. She wanted to feel joy about her success rather than the lonely, hollow feeling that rushed in at the end of each day. She wanted to have more energy to do things that interested her instead of going home to her usual half a bottle of Chardonnay and Netflix show.

I had been thinking about Toby outside of session. I'd been brainstorming ideas, allowing my thoughts of her to float in and out of my conscious mind. I brought some of those thoughts to her in this third session, and told her that a question someone had asked me recently had been popping up in my mind: "If a news crew called and told you they were outside your house and wanted to do an interview about your latest work, what would you scramble to change about yourself or your home?" She tried the question on and pondered a few answers for herself. She and I both agreed that we would make sure our clothes were appropriate—no pajamas or bathrobes. She also commented that she would close her bathroom door because she didn't want them seeing any part of her beauty regimen. I told her that my office desk was probably off limits because of the personal nature of some of the raw material with which I worked—both clients' and my own. We continued imagining with each other for about ten minutes.

Our conversation was quite divergent. We weren't working toward figuring out something specific; we were just having an open dialogue about a hypothetical situation. I didn't have an agenda in which this conversation was a numbered step to check off of the list. I was also contributing a lot of my own ideas that were different from the ones Toby was sharing. Allowing this kind of conversation to take place is a form of Incubating in session with a client. It is an act of holding that permissive stance. Thoughts don't have to be disciplined and analyzed;

they can be free to roam and weave with a client's thoughts. Often this leads naturally into an Initial Idea.

Sure enough, from our conversation, an idea did occur to me. I ended up inviting her to use paper and yarn to piece together a representation of how she looked from the inside. When I invited her to explore this invitation, she responded with eager curiosity. She may have thought the questions were strange, but I believe that because I had collaborated with her in the first stage of the creative process, she was able to be open to the subsequent stages.

This kind of open dialogue where we aren't focused on finding a specific solution can be somewhat confusing for clients. Many come to session expecting an interview that feels driven to find answers. I know this more open-ended, collaborative kind of conversation is important for my creative process. My clients often find it helpful too. So I taught Toby about divergent thinking and told her the ways in which I support my Incubating process. She was able to understand because she had a specific ritual that she used when starting a new interior design project. She told me that she would get her best ideas after taking a "virtual travel adventure." She would surf the web and pretend that she was planning a trip to an exotic location. She'd look at hotels from all over the world. She would read menus from local restaurants and imagine herself dressed to tour her vacation destination. Once she returned from her virtual trip, ideas would invariably have popped into her head and she would be ready to start her new project.

As she described her process and I reflected on our conversation, it came to me that this collaborative Incubation process was like pulling taffy. I shared this image with her: we stretched the ideas together as far as they could go, then wadded the taffy up, only to stretch it again in a different direction. Pretty soon we would make the taffy into actual pieces, but first we had to condition it to the right light and fluffy texture. From then on, whenever Toby got a quizzical look on her face because of my "strange but good questions," I would remind her about pulling taffy. She would nod with understanding and say, "Okay, let's go for it. Let's do some good taffy pulling."

Summary

Incubating is the necessary beginning of any creative endeavor. The divergent or "soft" thinking that Incubation requires prepares us to make new connections and come up with unique ideas for our work. There is no one right way to Incubate; each of us has to identify a way of Incubating that invites our minds to soften and find inspiration from unexpected sources. Incubating is not analysis, and is not aimed at finding a specific solution. It is permissive and dreamy, and asks us to use varied experiences outside of our work. When we trust and practice this stage of the creative process, we are preparing ourselves and our clients to successfully begin the second stage of the creative process and generate an Initial Idea.

Questions to Ponder

1. When is your mind most relaxed?
2. Do you tend to act on your first idea without generating options or brainstorming?
3. Do you bring a playful approach to your thinking or do you tend to lean more toward serious analysis?
4. Think of a time when you were clearly procrastinating on starting a creative endeavor (writing, making art, or thinking about a client). What did procrastination feel like for you?
5. Do you have activities that contribute to your "breadth of learning?" If so, what are they and how do they contribute to your ability to Incubate?
6. Do you let yourself think about clients outside of session in a productive way?
7. Do you invite clients to "pull taffy" with you? How might you do more of this and explain it to your clients?

Art Invitations

Incubating is the first step to being creative. It is the permission slip that allows you to be more fluid with your work. When you master this first stage of the creative process, you are well on your way to brilliantly navigating your way through any therapy session without getting stuck. You will think of ideas that are uniquely applicable to your specific client and feel liberated from the same old clinical blueprint. While it sounds exciting and attractive to approach your work creatively, it does take practice. You will need to gain an inherent trust in your creative process. In order to help you do this, I've included some art invitations that will help you practice the first stage of your creative process, Incubating.

Drips

This activity primes you for the other art activities by inviting you to experience art making as free and exciting. If you have any negative beliefs about your art ability, this activity should help. It is a beautiful mindfulness practice that helps everyone experience the stillness required to Incubate.

As discussed in Chapter 2, you may have some personal beliefs about art making. I often hear that there are family rules that govern who is or was the artist. These rules label people and define the excluded non-artists as lesser beings: "My mom was the artist. She was so beautiful and creative. I never felt worthy in her eyes because I couldn't paint like she did." "My sister was always the one expressing feelings. She did this in big, intrusive ways. I think that's what made her so good at art—access to all those overwhelming feelings. I stay away from feelings and art in order to avoid any of that awful stuff." These are a couple of examples I have heard.

So, as this is our first activity, I'm not going to invite you to just "paint something," because you might have beliefs about how your art is "supposed" to look. Instead, I'm going to invite you to make a drip painting. Dripped paint automatically defies preconceived notions about how art should look because it is absolutely random by nature. It just can't be controlled! When you start to interact with drips, watch how the drips travel and merge into other colors. If you don't watch closely (in other words, "stay in the present moment"), you miss amazing stuff! Colors turn corners, change direction, and pick up other colors. It becomes exciting to add new colors. Curiosity starts to override expectations. Negative beliefs no longer apply.

Here's what you need:

- Large paper (24" x 36")
- Water-based paint in a variety of colors
- Paint palette
- Paint brushes
- Water.

Here's how:

1. Water down a light color of paint to a fairly thin consistency, like milk, and use it to paint a background onto your paper. It doesn't have to dry in order for you to do the next step.
2. Choose a few colors of paint and put them into your palette. Make sure they are watery rather than the consistency of toothpaste.
3. Dip a brush into water first, then into paint. While standing the paper vertically or tacking it to a wall, start to apply the paint from the top of the paper. Let it drip.
4. Experiment with other colors. Feel free to turn the paper to make the drips create angles or turns. Just play. The key is watering down the paint enough so that it will travel.
5. Really pay attention and visually capture the moments when the drips change color and direction. An attitude of curiosity is key. Get excited about the little things. Remember, this is a totally random process that gives you permission to withhold judgment.

6. Take notes about your experience. What was exciting? What was new? What held your attention?

7. Answer this question: What new positive beliefs about art making and my creative process can I take away from this process/experience?

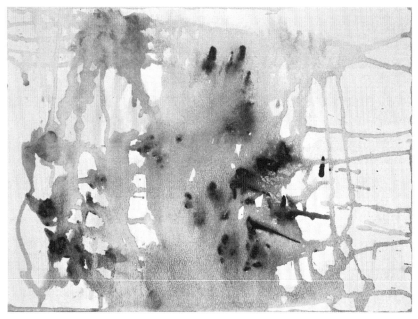

Figure 3.1 Ruth's "Drips"

Ruth noted: "I like watching the paint drip in a conscious way. It makes me think of my work with clients: if I can relax, [the work] just keeps going on a deeper and deeper level. I might not know the outcome, but if I can just go with the client, it is inevitably better."

Figure 3.2 Jamie's "Drips" (see color version in plate section)

Jamie observed: "I was seeing new possibilities at every turn and didn't have to be wed to one. The gentleness and trust that I could bring to this was so nice. I felt like it didn't have to be one way, and I could feel the freedom to think about the constant change. This trust is so important in doing our work. I can remind myself to stay with the drips, that the ideas will come if I can just trust."

Rainbow Breathing

Like "Drip Painting," Rainbow Breathing is a wonderful activity to help you find stillness and begin to tap into your creative process. This activity is one that I like to use with clients, too; this is described in Chapter 4. This experience helps to relax an over-analytic brain and provide some space for the divergent thought that is important in the Incubation stage of your creative process.

Here's what you need:

- Large paper (24″ x 36″)
- Water-based paint, marker, or other drawing medium in a variety of colors
- Paint palette (if using paint)
- Paint brushes (if using paint)
- Water (if using paint).

Here's how:

1. Practice breathing without the art first. A three-part breath is a good start. Breathe in through your nose, expanding your belly (low), then bring the breath into your mid-abdomen (middle), then all the way up to your chest (high). Exhale through your nose with the same emphasis, but in reverse (high, mid, low).
2. Move to your paper. Hold a dry brush or capped marker and track your breathing with your arm movement. Move your arm up as you inhale and down as you exhale. Stay present and focused on the dual nature of this experience, with an internal eye tracking your breath and an external eye watching your brush or marker. Relax and enjoy.
3. Now add your medium—paint, marker, etc.—and as you inhale, paint or draw a line all the way up the paper. As you exhale, paint or draw a line all the way down the paper. Change colors and repeat until you've filled the whole paper. Some people find that moving their arm in an arc (like a rainbow) feels more natural. However your arm moves, the many varied colors give a rainbow effect.
4. While looking at the lines that cover your paper, integrate your breathing experience. How does it feel? Did you allow your thinking to relax? What ideas, if any, pop into your head now?
5. Step away from the art and try calling up the color and line in your mind's eye. Start to breathe and access the visual experience. This is something that you can do whenever you need to—even if you don't have art materials available.

Figure 3.3 Vikki's "Rainbow Breathing"

As a result of doing this art activity, Vikki decided that she doesn't spend enough time doing this level of relaxed thinking about clients. She said, "I was so comfortable when I was painting and matching my breath. This activity really does facilitate open thinking for me."

Figure 3.4 Carol's "Rainbow Breathing" (see color version in plate section)

Carol really liked Rainbow Breathing because it slowed down her thinking. She said, "It got me out of that overthinking mode about what I am going to do. I could just enjoy it for what it is." She related this to thinking about clients in and out of session. "If I get out of myself and let it happen with clients, back away in my mind, then the Flow can come, and I am present."

Where Does It Belong?

This art activity asks you to use brainstorming as a way of Incubating an idea. The other two art activities in this chapter have helped you practice the relaxed, soft way of thinking that brainstorming requires. Once you've used your brainstorming, you will also be asked to continue with the art activity. It is a great exercise in choice making and a great introduction to the next stage of the creative process, Initial Idea.

Here's what you need:

- Magazine images
- Scissors
- Glue stick
- Drawing paper (large is better—18″ x 24″)
- Oil pastels, crayons, markers, or your preferred drawing material.

Here's how:

1. From the magazine image selection, choose an image that speaks to you as a starting point. You can choose any criteria for this image, or just let it choose itself.
2. Look at your image and ask yourself, *Where does it belong?* Imagine your image in an environment. What would it look like?
3. Take time to brainstorm at least four ideas about where your image belongs. If you like, you can write a list to help you remember.
4. Choose one of your ideas from step 3.
5. Glue your image onto the paper and draw your idea of where the image belongs. Give your image an environment.
6. Think about your process. Was brainstorming easy, hard, productive? How did you come up with your ideas?

Figure 3.5 Jamie's "Where Does it Belong?"

Jamie's brainstorming experience was validating for her. She realized
that the ideas in her list were related and all had the same essence. "This
realization simplified everything so that choosing wasn't an issue anymore,"
she said. As she drew the environment, she let the idea develop as she went
along and noticed that it went from very concrete to more metaphoric.
She connected this experience to the therapeutic setting and could see the
need to do this brainstorming for clients. "Letting ideas simmer there and
not taking them at face value is important. That pregnant pause really takes
us to important places with clients."

Figure 3.6 Christine's "Where Does it Belong?" (see color version in plate section)

Christine approached her dog image in a similar way that she would approach a client. She asked herself, "What's he feeling?" This question allowed her to start brainstorming ideas. Because she wanted to give him a safe environment, she started thinking of safe places that she could draw for him. She thought of a doghouse, a living room, and then a cave. She chose the cave because she had the sense that he was pulling himself in somewhere. Her relationship with her idea and her dog grew as she went along. She said of her Incubating experience, "It unfolded as I went along. My idea expanded, and I let it. I really see how my own inner world influences my creative process no matter what."

4

INITIAL IDEA

We have seen that the first stage of the creative process requires the cultivation of an open mind that is conducive to soft thinking. The second stage of the creative process, Initial Idea, marks the moment when, from this prepared state, our mind seizes an opportunity or an idea.

It is fairly common to see this part of the creative process included in the first stage. When Incubating and Initial Idea are combined, the first stage of the creative process is often referred to as "Inspiration." I feel it is important to delineate the Initial Idea from Incubating because it allows us to focus on the different and subtle aspects of each stage.

To understand the difference between Incubating and the Initial Idea, it might be helpful to think of a funnel. At the wide mouth of the funnel, we can imagine all of the brainstorming, breadth of learning, acts of meditative stillness, and taffy-pulling conversations with our clients. These divergent thoughts swirl around the top of the funnel and get mixed together in new ways as they travel down to the narrow straw at the bottom of the funnel. As these newly mixed thoughts travel down the funnel's straw, they converge and form a distilled idea. In this second stage, we are no longer engaging in rituals that facilitate a relaxed mind; instead we are refining our search and watching out for what might emerge from the end of the straw.

Seeing the Initial Idea emerge from the end of the straw is our "aha" moment. We can feel bright and clear, and curious. Often the "aha" will let us begin to approach the creative endeavor in a new light. We may not know exactly where that idea is going to lead us, but we have a much clearer sense of where to start.

Just as it is important to understand and practice Incubating, it is also important to understand and practice the act of finding an Initial Idea. We need to learn to fully embrace our Initial Ideas and simultaneously acknowledge that they are only starting points. The idea may not seem "right" or "good enough," but if we don't trust our Initial Idea, we end up blocked in our creative process. We need to approach our Initial Ideas with curiosity and celebrate times when they seem out of the box. When we bring an excitement to experiment to this stage of the creative process, we end up having unique inspirations that are wonderful catalysts for new discoveries and change. To trust that an Initial Idea will come, and to hone in on the moment when it does arrive, requires full partnership with our creative process.

The case studies, stories, and art invitations that follow are designed to illuminate the subtle awareness and convergent way of thinking that this second stage of the creative process requires.

The Planner

Margaret came to see me as an individual client because she felt her high level of anxiety was preventing her from being able to fully engage with her own clients on an emotional level. She was a new therapist, having come to the field after a 25-year career as a fifth-grade teacher. She had taught all of her working life, and at age 50, decided to go back to school and focus on something that would address the emotional difficulties with which she saw so many of her students struggle. Margaret dressed her athletic body in no-nonsense button-down shirts and chinos, which made it easy for me to imagine her as a competent schoolteacher. She had an intense gaze and slightly furrowed brow that let me know she was always thinking, always trying to figure things out. I had an affinity for her directness, but at times I found myself impatient with her anxiety. I heard myself encourage her to "just relax" many times in my head.

Margaret recognized the fact that being an effective therapist required her to tone down many of her classroom management skills and instead rely more heavily on her ability to establish a relationship with her clients. This was difficult for her. She became fearful when she couldn't rely on rules and structure. She wanted to be more creative and spontaneous, but didn't know if she had the ability. She was so unaccustomed to this discomfort that she began doubting herself as a therapist and was seriously wondering whether she was cut out for the job. "All I want to do is help," she told me, "but I can't seem to figure out what to do in session that would really make a difference. I end up tripping over my doubts instead of actually working on something with my clients."

It was clear to me that Margaret was having trouble in the second stage of her creative process. She was caught up with finding the very best Initial Idea, which blocked her from connecting in a creative and therapeutic way with her clients. Margaret needed to experience the act of being creative from start to finish and gain firsthand knowledge about the Initial Idea's role in the whole process. She needed to see that the Initial Idea was only a starting point and embrace the fact that she didn't have to be able to see where it would end up.

Margaret's passion was not lacking. She was intelligent, empathic, and determined. Her organizational skills had been put to good use in the classroom where her students consistently showed progress in all areas of learning. These same traits carried over into her work with me. She would arrive to her session, notebook in hand, enthusiastic and ready to learn. "What are we going to work on today?" she'd ask. When I introduced a topic of conversation or an art invitation, she'd want to know beforehand what these starting points were intended to teach.

When we talked about some of the clients with whom Margaret was working, she could tell me detailed histories and in-depth assessments about each of her clients. She had a list of treatment goals that she had carefully considered. She had generated many intervention ideas that sounded useful. But when it came down to actually picking a starting point, Margaret was frozen. She couldn't make up her mind and struggled to identify the very best Initial Idea. She wanted to be sure that whatever she chose to introduce in session would end up helping the client achieve one of the treatment goals. In her wish for certainty, she was stuck, and invariably ended up falling back on doing more assessment with her clients instead.

In our work, Margaret's approach to making art in session with me seemed to exacerbate her doubt. For instance, one day I invited her to represent a client for whom she'd expressed concern. She stared at the chalk pastel tray, unable to start. She was happy to brainstorm her ideas about what she might put on the page in order to represent the client's unstable living situation and self-harm. She told me she could make a picture with cyclone-shaped lines trying to balance on the wobbling point of a triangle. She imagined a bonfire that leapt off the page, a scribble that covered the entire page, and even a little frog with spots. I got excited and applauded her divergent thoughts. When I encouraged her to pick one of her Initial Ideas for her drawing—reminding her that doing this creative representation could help her look at her client from another perspective and possibly be able to identify interventions that would be helpful—Margaret went blank. Rather than choosing an idea and starting to draw it, she wanted to back up and spend more time thinking of a better, more applicable idea. She told me she wanted to be thorough and not leap to conclusions. She was paralyzed by her options. "Besides," she said, "I've never been able to draw what's in my head, so why even try?" Margaret lacked experience with her creative process. She relied heavily on her thought patterns and cognitive analysis and didn't trust her creativity.

Despite my best effort to coax Margaret into believing that the starting point was not the end point—that she needed to start somewhere in order for the creative process and the therapeutic process to take place—she was stuck.

I talked to her about other artists' creative processes and how they treated Initial Ideas. I told her that Picasso didn't take his starting points very seriously; instead, he was more interested in the ideas that came once he put his pen to paper. All he had to do was pick a starting point and trust that it would lead him somewhere new (Zervos, 1952). I encouraged her to get inspired by the way the painter Chuck Close stops himself from preconceiving his work, and instead just gets busy and lets things occur to him in the process. But teaching Margaret through these examples didn't seem to be getting us anywhere, either.

One day during this period, Margaret mentioned that she had been thinking about Dr. Iacabucci, a poetry professor from college, who had also overseen the poetry club which published a yearly poetry anthology. Margaret had fond memories of the club meetings and of writing poems for the anthology. She told me that her professor had a similar way of teaching to mine. He had banned her method of titling a poem before it was written, and had taught her that one phrase was enough from which to build a poem.

She became bright eyed and animated while telling me the story of the first poem she wrote in this way. She had just come back from a trip to the ocean with some friends where they had encountered wild elk. She had marveled at the impressions in the high grass that the elk had made during the night's rest and had returned with the phrase, "and the elk slept in their soft grass beds," which became the starting point for a poem she loved.

Margaret's excitement was beautiful. She loved the poem and the heightened creativity that writing it had exemplified. She admitted to me that she had many of these beginning phrases milling around in her head, but she never did anything with them. I was relieved and excited to find Dr. Iacabucci as an important resource in Margaret's endeavor to manage anxiety in the face of doubt. He had taught her the importance of starting, even if she wasn't certain where it would lead.

I began having Margaret practice engaging with her Initial Ideas by asking her to follow through with those phrases that she carried around. She brought the results into session to share. By her own admittance, some were good poems and some were failed attempts. But she was able to continue because she saw that, in the long run, starting a poem, even if it wasn't good, was better than not starting and having all the phrases in her head wasted.

Once Margaret had more of a handle on facing the unknown in her poetry, we began to talk about client sessions in the same way. Her fear of having a session end without important change or insight made this application more difficult, but nevertheless she was able to build some muscle in this area. She used her poetry practice as a model and decided that the phrases milling around in her head that related to clients were important. She couldn't just let the phrases stay in her head; she had to capture them and use them in some way to see where they could lead her and her client.

Often, the phrases that were loudest in her head were statements that led to more questions. For example, she had been trying to come up with some ideas to help a 17-year-old client who, despite an excellent academic record, was unable to complete college applications. Margaret recognized that this was related in part to her client's anxiety about being rejected from her first-choice college, but she sensed there was more going on. Margaret kept hearing herself say, "She's not dating." I suggested that she honor this phrase as an Initial Idea. I reminded her that she didn't need to know where it would lead, and instead of following her usual pattern of trying to find other, better ideas, she could ask her client about dating.

Margaret did, in fact, ask her client about dating. Acting on her Initial Idea in this way launched her into the third stage of her creative process, Diving In. She was no longer blocked in the second stage. She was truly partnering with her creativity. As a result, Margaret and her client moved to an entirely unexpected place. It turned out that her client had had a boyfriend for the last year. He had moved out of the state during the summer, only to leave Margaret's client with the emotional turmoil of having an abortion. Margaret's client hadn't told anyone but her boyfriend, who tried to support her from many states away. Together, Margaret and her client had unlocked the door to a host of emotional issues that had been keeping this client from moving forward. And Margaret once again saw the value of just starting somewhere despite not knowing where it would lead.

Margaret went from approaching her therapy like a teacher would—lesson plan in hand, results for every session listed—to approaching her therapy like an artist would. She had more trust in her ability to flow with things and allow them to develop as they needed in sessions. She respected her questions and ideas and used them with her clients as parts of the process. Margaret was less doubtful about her abilities as a therapist because she embraced the ambiguity that comes with the creative and therapeutic process. And best of all, Margaret was no longer stuck in the second stage.

The Importance of Finding an Initial Idea

The Initial Idea stage of the creative process is a bit like arriving at a trailhead for a hike. Incubating happens prior to arriving while we are gathering our gear, imagining what we might see on the hike, or are simply going about other non-hiking activities. When we arrive at the trailhead, we can see the sign that indicates where we are to start walking, and yet, we don't know exactly where the trail will lead. Even if we've been on the same hike many times before, we can't know what we will see, how it will feel, and exactly what it will look like when we arrive at our destination. In order for any hiking to happen, we must identify the trailhead as the place to start. Margaret learned to change her method of finding trailheads. Her old way of mapping out every possible trail that would get her to a specific destination had bogged her down. Rather than getting stuck in her research, Margaret learned to use a word phrase to find her trailhead. If we can't find an Initial Idea, we can't navigate the third stage of the creative process, Diving In. We have to have a starting point. Without one, we are blocked, and the therapeutic process and our creative process become stagnant.

What an Initial Idea Requires

An Initial Idea is a moment of clarity that can arrive in various forms—words, images, or sensory information. Incubating sets the groundwork for this moment of connection to happen. In order to identify the Initial Idea, we need to:

- Show up
- Tolerate ambiguity
- Give up certainty.

Show Up

When we practice capturing an Initial Idea, or finding the trailhead, we learn that this is accompanied by an internal sense of ideas falling into place. Many artists describe this as the feeling of solving a puzzle or finding the missing piece.

We have to hone our ability to monitor the arrival of an Initial Idea. That light-bulb moment is not something that we can passively await. Effective Incubation primes our thinking, but we also need to actively monitor our experiences for signs that our Initial Idea has arrived.

In my own creative process, I use the analogy of a loose tooth. When I was little and discovered I had a loose tooth, I was not at all willing to pull it before it was ready. I would go about my day with my tooth in the back of my mind, and every once in a while my tongue would give it a wiggle and check in on its progress. If the tooth wasn't ready to be pulled, I would go back to my other activities for a time. I would check on my tooth's readiness periodically for several days, until the time when my tongue determined that it was ready to come out.

Similarly, when I'm trying to figure out an Initial Idea for a client, a painting, or a writing piece, I let my soft thinking happen as I Incubate, and every once in a while I do a little check to see if my Initial Idea is ready. The check-in, like my tongue's assessment of a tooth, is an act of coming to the present moment to see where things stand. When we show up and do a check, we can be more active in finding those Initial Ideas.

It is not unusual for creative people, including the therapists who attend my workshops, to report a physical sensation that signals the arrival of an Initial Idea. They often describe finding an Initial Idea as an ease of tension that comes after much Incubating. Nietzsche's vivid description can help us understand the sense of relief that is often accompanied by the arrival of an Initial Idea: "Something profoundly convulsive and disturbing suddenly becomes visible and audible with indescribable definiteness . . . a thought flashes out like lightning, inevitably without hesitation" (Kelly and Kelly, 2007: pp. 445–6).

As therapists work to find Initial Ideas while making art in my workshops, I ask them to tune into the physical sensations that can indicate the moment when their Initial Idea comes into consciousness. When Margaret encountered the moment that she could show up for the phrase milling around in her head, she noticed that her surroundings looked brighter and her heart beat faster. Many, like Nietzsche, say the arrival of the Initial Idea feels like a lightning bolt of electricity. Some describe tingling in their limbs or at the backs of their necks. One of my favorites is the description an artist friend gave me: "It's like I'm breathing my first full breath of the day." Whatever the physical sensation, we need to be able to show up in the present moment in order to become aware that it is happening. Only then can we capture that Initial Idea.

Tolerate Ambiguity

Not all Initial Ideas are crystal clear. The physical sensations that accompany them can be clear, but the actual idea is often vague, nonverbal, or only an intuitive hunch. This can be unnerving for folks who like to explain the "why" of what they do in their work. But tolerating the ambiguous nature of Initial Ideas is something we need to learn to do. When we place value on these ideas, even when they are vague, we embrace the creative process and circumvent creative blocks.

While the Initial Idea is sometimes unclear, it almost always occurs in the context of a broader theory, treatment plan, or protocol. By remembering the bigger picture, you may be able to better tolerate the ambiguity. For instance, one time Margaret was working with a client whose sense of powerlessness prevented her from taking any steps toward improving her relationship with her elderly mother. As a result, this client was stuck in an unhealthy, codependent relationship that left her filled with guilt and resentment. Margaret had started to work toward the overall goal of helping her client identify strengths and internal resources. This gave Margaret a broad goal, but she was still looking for an Initial Idea of how to facilitate this experience for her client in session. Again, it was one of Margaret's phrases, "They are always with her," that cued her to this Initial Idea. Once she listened to the phrase, she had the Initial Idea. She didn't quite know how she was going to use it, but she knew it fit somehow. Rather than agonizing over it, she welcomed its ambiguity, reminding herself that it was just a starting point.

When her client arrived to her next session, Margaret had her unclear Initial Idea at the ready, and to her surprise, another Initial Idea came. Margaret's client plunked a huge handbag down onto the table and, in that instant, Margaret's vision became very bright. She connected her phrase, "They are always with her," to her client's handbag. From this Initial Idea, Margaret talked about her thoughts with her client and entered the third stage of the creative process—Diving In. It turned out that Margaret's client always carried many important resources and representations of strength in her purse. Together they admired the locket that her best friend had given her, which housed a picture of her as a new mother and affirmed her worth as a mother and friend. They laughed at the baby wipes and the snack food (her purse was quite big) and celebrated the preparedness that these items represented. The pile of items from the purse grew, and at the end of the session there was a felt experience of the resources that the purse contained and represented. Had Margaret forced her Initial Idea into clarity, she might not have been able to seize the moment of connection between her Initial Idea phrase and her client's purse. Because she had been able to tolerate the ambiguity, Margaret and her client were able to Dive In and make significant strides toward identifying strengths and resources.

Give Up Certainty

Linda was a seasoned art therapist who participated in an off-site retreat that I facilitated for her agency. She came to the retreat burnt out and feeling stuck in her work. When she introduced herself to the group, I could hear the pressure she put on herself to be a good therapist. She referred to multiple theoretical approaches in which she was very well versed— EMDR, Somatic Experiencing, Dialectical Behavior Therapy, and Neuro-Linguistic Programming. She could rattle off various directives that she used and was clearly very competent, yet she described her sessions as "hollow and colorless." She said she felt like she was deciding what the session would look like according to the progress note that she had to write for county billing. This felt lifeless to her and not very effective for her clients. She wanted to get back to her roots as an art therapist and feel like she believed in the creative process again. Early in the day, she admitted, "If I don't breathe some vibrancy into my work, I'm not sure I can keep it up. And I'm absolutely sure my clients won't keep coming."

For the first art activity, I invited her to make a representation of the stagnant feeling she had described about her work. I wanted to see what her nonverbal experience looked like. Linda responded to the art invitation by creating a collage. She printed out black-and-white images of her office, a professional portrait, and some of her own artwork. She equated these colorless images with the actions she felt she had to go through in order to get county reimbursement. She had to "look good" on paper, and she reduced her office experiences to this linear formula. She gave her clients a certain art directive or therapeutic activity because she knew it was supposed to satisfy the treatment goal that she was trying to achieve for the paperwork. She was emphasizing the end product, the thing that the client was supposed to take away, before her clients even engaged in the art activity. "I feel no more inspired than this drab-looking picture of my art table," she said.

I then invited Linda to use her nondominant hand and bring in some color to her art. I was curious about the difference for her. She started adding yellow lines in a sun pattern. They radiated out onto the black-and-white photographs. Soon the sun turned into a face, and she used her fingers to complete a self-portrait of herself at a younger age. She was quiet as she finger-painted, raising her eyebrows every once in a while at what appeared to be something funny or joyful. When she was done, she looked up at me with a big smile on her face. "I have to bring that color into session," she said. "It's so fun and bright."

I asked her to think about how this could guide her with her clients. "I need to remember there isn't a direct line between start and finish of a session," she replied. "Look how my art changed! I need to remember that the purpose of a directive is simply to get things started. It can change many times during a session. And who am I to think I can figure that out before I even see my client?"

Linda's blocked experience shows us what can happen when we try to forecast the therapy session and assume that an Initial Idea will take the session where we want it to go. After her work during the retreat and some follow-up sessions, she was able to give up her need for certainty. Instead, she embraced the mystery and brought radiant color back into her sessions.

How to Get Better at Finding Your Initial Idea

Since it can look so different for everyone, the following stories and concepts illustrate how we can more effectively navigate the second stage of the creative process and identify the arrival of an Initial Idea.

Befriend Beginnings

Cultivating a receptive stance toward Initial Ideas requires developing a healthy relationship with beginnings. Some people treat beginnings like they are no big deal, just a part of a day's work. A new project might be just another one to complete in a long line and its starting is less important than its finishing. A new client is just another relationship to be established and another person to begin to understand. Some people go in and out of beginnings without even noticing.

Others fear beginnings; they freeze up and avoid them. A new project fills them with stress hormones and they enter a state of procrastinating angst. They can't seem to move ahead with things that might lead to wonderful outcomes. Learning new skills, establishing new relationships, or initiating potentially confrontational conversations with clients doesn't happen. Some people dread new beginnings and can't seem to stop thinking about them.

Whether minimizing or catastrophizing beginnings, neither end of the spectrum is helpful when we are striving to live creative lives and inspire others to do the same. Instead, we need to find a relationship with beginnings that can remind us of the exciting possibilities and extraordinary surprises that await.

We need to practice what artists practice: the act of treating a beginning like an opening, a new horizon, a path that reveals itself only as you step onto it.

Court "Perfect Danger"

The concept of "perfect danger" resonates as a key to identifying a promising Initial Idea. In his book of blessings, "For the Artist at the Start of the Day" (2008), poet and philosopher John O'Donohue writes, "When we place profound trust in the act of beginning, we are making risk our greatest ally." The Initial Idea marks the beginning of a creative project; if we begin with an idea that feels a bit risky, it means that we don't quite know where it will take us. We are prepared to see and experience new things.

Artists practice refining what I like to refer to as their "danger gauge." This is a cleverly calibrated instrument that tells them precisely when they have approached perfect danger. Too little risk, and their Initial Idea has little new to offer—it's probably a repetition of something already known or discovered. Too much risk and the artist finds it difficult to sustain the necessary trust and effort to see a project through.

But the perfect danger—that's when artists feel they are being led by an invisible muse. Their physical reaction to an Initial Idea is intense, but not too intense. They feel excited and curious. They have a sense of being in tune with the process. Their intuition says go left and simultaneously their brush goes left as they feel as if they are up to something good.

The perfect danger can also happen when a therapist has a light-bulb moment and decides to invite a client to step out into new content, maybe material that has been avoided before that moment. The therapist doesn't know how the client will respond and might feel a strong sense of curiosity and excitement accompanying the idea. This idea invites the therapist and client to walk new ground together. In its newness, this "perfect danger" inspires growth and invites possibilities.

Each one of us has the potential to acquire a gauge inside that is calibrated to "perfect danger." We've had to use it in order to learn new things like crawl and walk and ride a bike. We've had to use it to embark on new career paths and start businesses. We have used it to achieve goals that we may never have worked toward had we not assessed the Initial Idea that was our "perfect danger." When we establish this gauge, we find a relationship between trust and risk. An idea to try a totally different approach with a client can feel risky because we don't know how it will go or what our clients' reactions will be. However, our gauge can guide us into embracing the Initial Idea because we know there is goodness, necessity, even perfection in the risk. The "perfect danger" tells us to honor the Initial Idea and use it. It reminds us to trust the process even in the face of uncertainty.

When we practice finding our Initial Idea in the context of doing creative activities like art, writing, or dancing, we get to tune into our gauge. We can use it intentionally and invite it to drive our creative process. We get to experience that spectrum between too little risk and too much risk, and then eventually calibrate a sweet spot where we find our "perfect danger."

Don't Operate Alone: Collaborate

My great aunt, Barbara Morgan, was a well-respected American photographer. The summer I turned 16, after a family dinner, I heard her tell the story of how she collaborated with the great modern dancer, Martha Graham. Her story taught me the power of working in relationship. It speaks to the collaborative nature of our work with clients.

My aunt wanted to capture the essence of the dancer. She knew that finding the right gestures was an essential element to her photographs, but she also knew if she asked Martha Graham to simply hold a certain pose or gesture, it wouldn't tell the whole story. The external gesture would be captured on film, but the internal state wouldn't accompany it. So my aunt decided that she would proceed a bit differently.

She attended the live performances of Martha Graham and Company multiple times, making notes about the dance sequences that most moved her (Initial Ideas). Later, she and Martha would go over the list of these passages. Then, on another day, Martha would come to my aunt's studio. Each woman brought her unique set of skills, the dancer and the photographer ready to join in a true collaborative master-piece. The minute they entered the room, they silenced them-selves. They didn't want words to distract from the moment.

Martha got in front of the camera, Barbara behind the cam-era. Barbara signaled Martha to begin one of the sequences. My aunt showed me the conductor's pose that began the sequence—hand held out in front of her raised eyebrow, index finger slowly meeting her thumb, slight lilt in her arm. Then they proceeded. Martha danced her fluid expressions of story and emotion. Barbara captured instants of timeless beauty and raw energy.

Their collaboration started with Barbara's Initial Idea for a photograph, but didn't stop there. They considered each set of sequences a new collaboration. It led to new Initial Ideas and then to the other stages of the creative process. Martha found her rhythm and grace, and Barbara found the stills to match. If either of them had approached the Initial Idea on their own, the process would have been totally different. Together they created a unique work of art.

The relationship that my aunt described between dancer and photographer is no different than the collaborative rela-tionship between client and therapist. We therapists bring our ideas, assessments, and questions to session, but they are noth-ing without the client's contribution. The creation of the thera-peutic relationship is collaborative. We must emphasize the dual exchange of verbal and nonverbal communication. In this way, together, therapist and client create unique works of art as unique and vibrant as Barbara Morgan and Martha Graham's stunning black-and-white photographs.

Follow the Rhythm Until it Changes

Years ago, I attended a workshop facilitated by art therapist, author, and professor, Shaun McNiff. It was around the time that his book, *Art as Medicine* (1992), had been published and I was just stepping into awareness of my creative process. He began his workshop with an art activity. While he walked around the room playing his thumb harp, he asked us to allow our bodies to make repetitive movements to start our painting. In response to his deliciously compelling upbeat harp rhythms, my arm danced in a round-and-round motion with the brush, my mind elsewhere. As he played, he chanted, "Don't stop the motion. Just keep with the rhythm." His music and his enthusiasm kept me curious. I wasn't tempted to stop and think about my painting; I only wanted to follow my arm and the blue circles that were unfolding on the page. His rhythm never changed. "Eventually," he told us, "your movement is going to change, even in the littlest way. This will change the look of the painting. In that moment, you've released yourself from the repetitions and launched yourself into an exciting endeavor."

Sure enough, that moment of change marked the beginning of a painting for me. The circles and the rhythm had facilitated my Incubation, and the slight shift marked the arrival of an Initial Idea. Without my knowing, my arm had started to square off the top edges of the circle and when Shaun reminded us to pay attention, I became acutely aware of the shift. No longer was my motion round and round. Instead, my brush was making a rounded square. My mind followed my brush, and I had the flash of an idea. Accompanied by the magic tinkling of a thumb harp, I started to make more squared-off circles and fit them together. I was making a rock wall. Eventually, my page was filled with the hand-shaped rocks that joined invisibly to make the wall that encircles my grandparents' property in Inverness, CA. I was celebrating my father who constructed the wall as my head moved in time with the thumb harp. I was transported back to the magical winter when the whole family put notes in the rock crevices as New Year's wishes.

Our thoughts can be like those blue circles. They can go round and round, and we can feel like we'll never get a moment of clarity. The Initial Idea can feel very far away. But when we watch out for the subtle change in movement, we have the chance to grab onto something. With the smallest alteration, our Initial Idea can come rushing in as if it had just been waiting for us to notice.

It is easy to get caught in a repetitive cycle without paying attention to the subtleties. My experience with Shaun McNiff taught me that it doesn't take much to notice the change. And the reward for noticing is often a wonderful Initial Idea.

Narrow Choices

It is not uncommon to have more Initial Ideas than can possibly be implemented. A flood of ideas can be exciting, but this can also feel overwhelming. While some therapists get stuck because they don't know which Initial Idea will lead to certain success (like Margaret), others do just the opposite. Rather than sitting with options, measuring for "perfect danger," and collaborating with their clients, therapists like Sophia (see below) used each and every Initial Idea in an enthusiastic, yet haphazard way. When this happens, we need to develop some criteria that help us to narrow our choices and prevent our creative process from getting bogged down in this stage.

Sophia was an upbeat and eager participant in my six-month intensive Creativity Seminar. A newly licensed therapist, she had joined me and seven other therapists for an intense look into her creative process. She welcomed the in-depth look at how her creativity influenced her therapeutic work. Sophia described herself as a very creative person. A dancer and painter, she longed to bring more of herself into her work with clients. However, she felt that the pressures of her work at a foster family agency made it difficult. Sophia seemed to drag herself to my studio. Her graceful dancer clothes draped in tandem with the hair that hung in her face. "I've been reduced to progress reports and quarterly assessments," she said in our first meeting. "There's no art to my work anymore."

Sophia told the group that she had at least a hundred unfinished paintings in her garage and enough ideas to start a thousand more. This part of her didn't seem to be dampened. Exuberant and passionate about the art invitations in the seminar, she was always the first one to jump into the project. The other participants admired her spirit and enthusiasm for everything.

In exploring her creative process, Sophia recognized the fact that she had no problem coming up with her Initial Idea in art and with clients. "It's like I'm constantly Incubating about everything and ideas just pop into my head all over the place," she said. This was a good sign that she was thinking creatively, but I was concerned that she might be too quick to act on her ideas.

I asked her about how she chose what to work on in session with a client. She thought for a moment and said, "Whatever idea is most current in my mind—I just search around in my head, find a clue about a topic or technique or something, then use it." She trusted her Incubation time so much that she felt sure her mostly preverbal idea would be a good starting point. She was the complete opposite of Margaret, who had worried about finding the very best idea. "In the end," said Sophia, "it doesn't really matter what you start with because it's about following the thread to where you end up anyway."

Sophia had embraced not-knowing in her art process and her therapy process in a very broad way, the result of which was a fairly haphazard approach to both. It is very true about the creative process that the end point will likely be very different from the starting point. However, Sophia seemed to be rushing the process of finding an Initial Idea. It was as if she was just snatching an idea from her brainstorm list at random. They all sounded good, so rather than considering them further, she started impulsively. Sophia was missing parameters on her Initial Ideas. As we tracked her process, we discovered that many of her ideas were preverbal hunches that she hadn't spent enough time filtering through her knowledge base to clarify.

I imagined her funnel of ideas and shared this with her. "It's like all of your ideas are swirling around at the top of the funnel," I explained, "and rather than waiting to see which one gels at the bottom of the straw, you're randomly picking an idea from the swirls at the top." Sophia needed to learn to bring some of her knowledge about treatment planning, therapeutic goals, and her clients' presenting issues into the decision. In other words, she needed to learn to make connections between her Initial Idea and her clients' unique needs.

As a new therapist, Sophia needed to learn to place some limits on her flood of ideas in much the same way a composer places creative parameters on a song to help guide the writing process. A composer might choose to write a piece for a particular set of instruments or decide to write within a sonata form and break the themes into different time signatures. In much the same way, some writers start with a framework in the form of a writing genre, a theme, and even an outline. With these limitations, an artist can refine her inspiration.

Sophia needed to learn to place this same kind of structure onto her Initial Ideas. If she could set a framework and refine the way she listened to her ideas, she would be more effective in therapy. She already had the ability to be free and open to many ideas, but she needed to slow down and choose less impulsively. We worked to set some criteria for her Initial Ideas. First, she would become more conscious of them by naming them rather than letting them stay preverbal. While she didn't like this because it didn't come naturally, she began to see that giving her ideas a bit of verbal form helped her refine many and even eliminate some.

The second parameter Sophia set up for herself was that when she had an Initial Idea or hypothesis about a client, she would ask herself, "Why now?" If her response was from her old pattern—"Because it's what's on my mind right now"—she made herself look for another answer. If her answer tied into a treatment goal, she used it. If she couldn't tie it in, she looked for ways that it could apply, but she didn't use the idea until she could see the connection.

By placing parameters on her Initial Idea, Sophia shifted her relationship to her creative process. She had formerly been too trusting and unconscious, and had flung herself into acting on her ideas before giving them any consideration. This had made her sessions feel disconnected from week to week, and once she saw this, she was sure that her clients would benefit from the continuity that her criteria could provide. With the criteria we set, Sophia was able to slow herself down so that she could make more of her ideas. Her sessions felt more related, and she felt clearer and more carefully artful than she had in the past. She was also clearer about her paperwork, and, as a result, felt less burdened by it.

Initial Idea with Clients

We have explored the importance of seizing the moment that our Initial Idea becomes clear, how it feels, and how we can use it as the start of the third stage of our creative process, Diving In. However, if our Initial Idea is our trailhead, that doesn't necessarily mean it is our client's, too. Talking about our idea in a collaborative and inviting way offers the very real potential to inspire our client to think of additions or alterations to our idea, or even to have his or her own Initial Idea. This often happens to me when I present an art invitation to a client. Sometimes my invitation resonates perfectly, but many times it does not. Because I encourage collaboration and embrace not knowing what will come of the Initial Idea, the client is free (and many times excited) to contribute new thoughts to my idea. In that exchange, we arrive at another starting point together.

One precious example of this collaboration was a session with Emily, a very expressive nine-year-old girl who didn't like to be told no. Her tantrums and disruptive behavior were a serious issue at home and at school. I felt that while sometimes these were attempts to manipulate others into saying yes, Emily also had little experience with self-soothing and other emotional regulation skills. I decided to teach her to breathe deeply in response to her upset feelings so she could slow down her reaction time.

My Initial Idea was to coach her to use a paintbrush at the end of her extended arm to represent her inhale and exhale. Before we added any paint to the activity, we practiced tracing the brush up the page as she inhaled, and then drawing it back down again as she exhaled. In her dramatic style, Emily began dancing her breath, arm swooping up and then down with brush in hand.

When I invited her to add paint once she had mastered the pretend "painting breath," she declared her Initial Idea and said, "I'm going to do Rainbow Breathing!" And she commenced making beautifully long inhales and exhales that arched, rainbow-style, across the page. Her arches were graceful, mesmerizing, and vibrant. Her breathing stayed in rhythm the whole time. I had introduced the Initial Idea, and Emily had collaborated to make it her own. We were the perfect creative team in that session. And, because Emily added her special touch, I believe that it boosted her ability to utilize Rainbow Breathing when she needed it. Emily even taught her parents to Rainbow Breathe, and the whole family adopted a new coping skill. (See the Art Invitations in Chapter 3 for a more detailed description of this exercise.)

Summary

The moment that our mind gleans an idea from the multitude of possibilities our Incubation has created, the second stage of the creative process, Initial Idea, has been navigated. This requires that we use convergent thinking to narrow our choices and notice the "aha" moment when new combinations are brought to light. This moment is often nonverbal and accompanied by a physical response. We can feel bright and clear, and curious. And, even though we may not know exactly where that idea is going to lead us, we feel a sense of relief because we have a much clearer idea of where to start with our creative endeavor. It is vital that we are ready for this moment. We need to stay alert so as not to miss it. It can also be a wonderful thing to collaborate on our Initial Idea with our clients. This collaboration can enrich the therapeutic process and make sessions feel more unique and spontaneous.

Questions to Ponder

1. How are you with beginnings?
2. How do you relate to starting something without being sure where it will end?
3. Think of a time when you experienced the light-bulb moment of an Initial Idea. What was it like? How did it feel?
4. Can you sense when you are about to come to an Initial Idea? What is this like? If not, think about where and when you get ideas. Start to notice, in real time, how these moments feel.
5. Have you experienced collaboration with your client on an Initial Idea? If so, how did it go? If not, what would it take for you to give it a try?

Art Invitations

Follow the Rhythm Until it Changes

This is the art activity that I described above. It's a fun activity to help you hone your ability to notice the opening—to really get clear about when that change in movement ushers in a new idea.

Here's what you need:

- Drawing paper
- Drawing material: pen, pencil, oil pastels, etc.

Here's how:

1. Play some music with an upbeat rhythm. Choose a song that will give you three to four minutes of listening time.
2. While listening to the music, let your arm start a movement. Stay with this movement and match it to the music rhythm.

3. Keep doing the repetitive movement while watching for any small change.
4. When you see the change in movement happen, make a note of the feeling, the experience, and become aware of any ideas that get spurred because of this change.
5. Keep making the changed movement until an Initial Idea arrives.
6. Continue working on your drawing by using your Initial Idea as a starting point.

Figure 4.1 Robin's "Follow the Rhythm Until it Changes" (see color version in plate section)

Robin said, "When [the Initial Idea] came to me, I felt it was too complicated, so I had to just keep going, trying to grapple with it, but also continue with my drawing. Then I came up with another thought that was a simplified version of the first one. It was whimsical, too. So I used it." She reflected that she often feels the need to modify an idea so that it isn't too complicated. If she throws out the idea before she can sort through it, she gets lost. With this art experience, she decided she would stay with an idea, even if it felt too difficult or overwhelming, and see if she could simplify it.

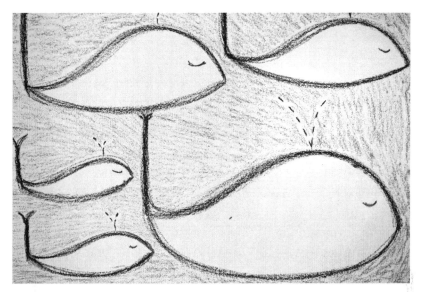

Figure 4.2 Carly's "Follow the Rhythm Until it Changes"

Carly's experience helped her recognize and understand the moment of mental tension right before an idea arrives. "I followed the movement, even when I didn't know where it was going. It felt like it was building and building, and then I could feel the shift happen. I looked at it, and all of a sudden it was a whale. I was blown away". She decided that she wanted to practice intentionally staying with the tension and asking herself, "What wants to happen here?" instead of forcing ideas to happen.

Only Five Words

Word play can be helpful when trying to arrive at an Initial Idea. Any time we are able to see something externally, it brings a new perspective on our internal thoughts and states. I like to use magazine words to help me see the thoughts that are going round and round in my head. When you start with defining the problem, then play with the words you've chosen, new connections can bring clarity to the Initial Idea.

Here's what you need:

- Magazine words (a large variety—I keep a shoebox full)
- Glue stick
- Paper.

Here's how:

1. Start by finding words that you associate with your client. These can be about the presenting problem, ways you might describe your client, things you know about your client, etc. Don't limit the number of words that you pick at this point. Just allow yourself to respond to the words you see. You don't even necessarily have to be able to explain why you've picked the words.

2. Arrange the words so that you can read them all at once. Begin to pick words that "define the problem." This is a vague term meant for your soft-thinking brain. You don't need to analyze or understand yet. Use as many words as you need.

3. If you have more than five words chosen at this point, eliminate words until you are left with only five. Glue these five words on the paper.

4. Now that you have refined the "problem," you likely see it from a different perspective. You can now use this perspective to come up with an idea or hypothesis about what you might work on in sessions to come. You may not come up with an idea right away. This is an exercise in seeing from a different perspective. Read the words out loud and allow the Initial Idea to emerge.

5. Write down your new perspective or the connection that you made and keep it handy as a stepping-stone to accessing other new ideas.

(a)

Figure 4.3a Brenda's "Only Five Words" Steps 1 and 2

Brenda picked words that reminded her of a teen client with whom she'd been working for a few months. Her client's emotional outbursts caused a great deal of distress for her family and teachers and Brenda had become overwhelmed with trying to help intervene.

(b)

Figure 4.3b Brenda's "Only Five Words" Step 3

When Brenda chose her five words, she was able to see a different perspective. "The Awesome Storm Inside is something that I've been really missing in my work with this client. I've been so focused on putting out the fires that I've neglected what is causing these fires." As a result, Brenda decided that in addition to the parenting support she was providing, she was going to capture the Initial Idea that her words helped her see. "I'm going to work a lot more with my client on helping her express and regulate the intense emotion that seems to be fueling her acting out."

Figure 4.4a Susan's "Only Five Words" Steps 1 and 2

Figure 4.4b Susan's "Only Five Words" Step 3

Susan's client desperately wanted a new start and came to therapy after the prolonged illness and eventual death of her husband. They had been doing some grief work that felt important, but Susan wanted to use her words to ascertain whether there was something she had neglected to bring into session. "My five words helped me think about my client differently. We had been working a lot on her experience as her husband's caretaker as well as the grief and loss she felt. I hadn't thought to *highlight forgotten experience.*" As a result of her art activity, Susan had the Initial Idea to look back at her client's life and celebrate who she was before her husband got sick. She was excited to do this and felt it was an important Initial Idea that could help her client with a new start.

NOW! Watch

Because Initial Ideas pop into our heads outside of session, it is helpful to have an external reminder to check for them. Sometimes we enjoy divergent thought and forget to check if anything has gelled. Staying in touch with the rhythm of checking on thoughts is vital to capturing the Initial Idea.

A NOW! watch can be a great reminder to do a check to see if an Initial Idea has arrived. We check our watches for the time, but a NOW! watch can change that habit and tell us to check for an idea.

Here's what you need:

- An old watch with a fairly large face (go to thrift stores and snap up the cool ones that don't work)
- Heavy paper—watercolor or other 120 lb. paper (postcards or shirt boxes could work too)
- Markers, lettered ink stamps, computer fonts, magazine letters (some way for you to write the word "NOW!")
- Glue
- Beads or gems of some kind if you want to add a bit of sparkle.

Here's how:

1. First take apart your watch face by removing the backing and internal workings. Trace the glass face onto your paper to get the shape and size you will be working with.
2. Write or glue the word NOW! on the paper. Make it colorful, fun, interesting.
3. Insert your paper into the watch face (you can add a few beads at this time if you like) and then replace the backing of the watch.
4. Extra fun—add strings of beads to replace the existing band.
5. Practice using your NOW! watch. Think of a problem, Incubate on the problem, and every once in a while, look down at your

watch to bring yourself into the present moment to check on connections. You can do this same rhythm in session. As you are engaging with your client and the session is going along, every time you look at your NOW! watch, ask yourself if there are other connections being made. You may even want to ask your client to join you in this rhythm.

Figure 4.5 Group's NOW! Watches (see color version in plate section)

A group on a retreat had a wonderful time making and wearing their NOW! watches. Throughout the retreat, I would ask, "What time is it?" When I did, they looked at their watches and checked in with their reflections and potential ideas about the art activity I had assigned.

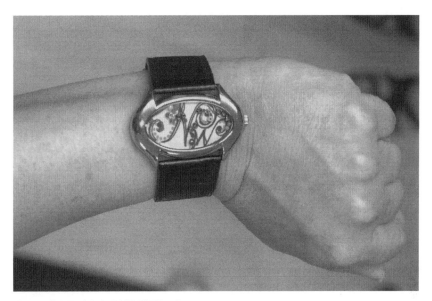

Figure 4.6 Robin's NOW! Watch

Robin told us she was going to use her NOW! watch to help her remember to check on ideas that were unfolding in and out of session. She said, "Sometimes I get so far ahead of myself. This is going to be a helpful reminder that my thoughts are always going. All I have to do is remember to become aware of them."

5

DIVING IN

The third stage of the creative process is a stage of action. While the first and second stages (Incubating and Initial Idea) require us to think, Diving In requires us to do something with that thinking. When we have successfully cultivated the divergent thinking of Incubation and subsequently captured an Initial Idea through convergent thinking, it is time to enter the third stage. Diving In means becoming more visible to ourselves and others because we externalize our thoughts and put them into action. At this stage in art making, we begin to create—putting brush to canvas, chisel to marble, pen to paper. At this stage in therapy, we begin the process of change—confronting, challenging, employing techniques, inviting new experiences, supporting expression. This stage of our creative process can feel vulnerable as we initiate our art, but it can also feel exhilarating as we respond authentically to our Initial Idea.

It can be helpful to understand this stage by imagining a hot summer day by the pool. Let's imagine that someone is reclining poolside, soaking in the sounds of children playing in the water. She feels relaxed and enjoys the summer sun. Her mind wanders to a recent art exhibit she attended, then to the meal she is going to bring to a sick friend, then to the color of her closed eyelids as the bright sunlight shines through. All of a sudden, our sunbather has an Initial Idea. A crystal clear thought brings her to the present moment and an idea converges in her mind. She thinks, *I must get cooled off in the pool.* Once she notices this idea, she decides that it is something she needs to act on, so she gets up and walks to the edge of the pool. The water is clear and inviting. Her feet feel the hot concrete and long to be immersed in the water. But she hesitates because she knows her dive is going to jar the warmth of her body. She knows from prior experience that it will feel good once she takes the plunge, but it takes a moment for her to brace herself for this change. And then, in another instant, she Dives In headfirst to the coolness, welcoming the refreshing sensation of water all around her.

It is helpful to remember that during the course of a summer, the swimmer will go through this Diving In process many, many times. Some days she will have an easy time of it at the edge of the pool. Other days, perhaps when the weather isn't as warm, she will have a harder time. But she will continue to Dive In.

When we do Dive In with our Initial Idea, we really are taking a plunge. Like the swimmer, we can't stand at the edge of the pool forever gathering courage. We can only dip our toe into the water to test the temperature so many times. Diving In can feel scary, exciting, exhilarating, and difficult all at once. We can desire the cool refreshing water as much as we are repelled by the shock of cold it will bring. To Dive In to our creative process, we have to be able to hold these disparate feelings and proceed anyway. Even when we don't know how our painting will turn out, how our client will respond, whether our creative process will have the end result we desire, we have to proceed and Dive In. Otherwise we are stuck in the creative process, and our clients will be stuck as well.

For every artist, Diving In is a test of authenticity. If we do not Dive In with our Initial Idea, we betray ourselves. We halt our creative process and become blocked. We must be able to act despite our fear of saying something the client doesn't want to hear. When we think of unconventional ideas or use interventions for the very first time, we must be able to act despite our fear of messing up. Our willingness to take the plunge, to show up and take action, exhibits respect for our creative process and for ourselves. When we squelch ideas out of fear or the need to conform, we end up on the side of the pool looking longingly at the water rather than delighting in the experience. In that sense, we disengage ourselves from the process of therapy and become bystanders who merely pay lip service to change. When therapists learn to Dive In despite the fear of uncertainty, we invite our clients to do the same.

The following stories, vignettes, and case studies further describe the challenge of Diving In. They highlight the dual nature of taking action—the fear of not knowing and the exhilaration of taking the plunge. When we are able to take action and implement our Initial Idea, we are truly immersed in the creative process. We are ready to grapple with the fourth stage, Flexible Commitment, and are well on our way to Flow.

Stuck on Nice

Marilyn had a warm, grandmotherly presence that I immediately loved. She arrived to my creativity retreat for therapists bearing the gift of a pile of old *National Geographic* magazines to add to my collage bin. The others in the retreat gravitated toward her because of her sweet demeanor and the genuine interest she showed in them. I could imagine how easily she established rapport with her clients and how fond of her they must be.

As Marilyn described to the group why she was attending the creativity retreat, it became clear to me that she was having trouble navigating the third stage of her creative process. She related a situation with a teen client with whom she thought she had been doing really well when his mother decided to send him to a different therapist. Marilyn felt blindsided because she had cared about the client and thought she had created a great working relationship with him, but his mother didn't think her son was making progress. This wasn't the first time that this had happened to Marilyn, and she wanted to understand her part in the problem.

Marilyn completed the Creative Process Assessment (Chapter 2) and decided that she wasn't as good at navigating any of the stages as she wanted to be. She was able to complete the scribble drawing in the assessment, and actually ended up enjoying it in many ways. But when I inquired further, it turned out that Marilyn had controlled her creative process in a very specific way. She had felt okay about the first two stages (Incubating and Initial Idea), and had been able to do both. But when it came time to actually act upon her Initial Idea, she spent time searching for an idea that felt safe to her. She had brainstormed many different ideas, but she could only embrace the ones that were positive and that she thought could yield something she liked in her drawing. She admitted to having "weird" or "different" ideas but she felt she couldn't act on these for fear of not liking the end result. Marilyn wasn't blocked in finding Initial Ideas; she could generate many. She was, however, blocked in acting on them because she limited herself to certainty and safety when deciding how to Dive In. This pattern was halting her creative process because she wasn't taking risks and letting go of her expectations. She was prioritizing comfort and the status quo—and stifling her creativity in the process.

In talking further about Marilyn's work, we were able to see a similar pattern in therapy to what she experienced in the assessment. She took Incubation time to consider ways that she could connect with all of her clients, particularly resistant ones. She did Dive In to this process with her new ideas and they helped her to forge pleasant connections with her clients. This part of her creative process was natural and enjoyable to her, just as she had experienced with her scribble drawing. But Marilyn's more confrontational and directive ideas, aimed at creating behavioral changes in the clients, were difficult for her to embrace.

Marilyn was able to describe one of those more challenging ideas for the client she had just lost. He tended to criticize his peers and deflect responsibility for the disappointing friendships he experienced. This led him to withdraw, isolate, and feel highly negative about his future. Marilyn's idea was to confront him about the kind of one-sided friendships he set up. She wanted to suggest that he bring in one of his friends to have a conversation about how her client made it difficult for a reciprocal friendship to exist.

As in her scribble assessment, Marilyn had the Initial Idea, but she hadn't acted on it because it didn't feel safe. She told me, "I was afraid he wouldn't like the idea and then he wouldn't be as comfortable with our relationship or want to come to therapy anymore. After all the time we spent on building the relationship, I didn't want to risk ruining it." Marilyn took her fear as a negative sign and, like she had with her scribble drawing, she squelched the more challenging, risky idea. In so doing, she had squelched her client's progress, too.

Often, the moment of Diving In does feel risky. It is the act of breaking the status quo; we don't know what is going to happen. Marilyn needed to work on her ability to tolerate the fear that came with implementing her ideas. I wanted her to understand how vital to the therapeutic relationship it was for her to lift her automatic censorship and be more authentic with her clients.

Diving In, for Marilyn, meant going beyond her ability to establish rapport and seizing the moment when she felt the need to confront or challenge her client. Rather than being stuck because of her need to minimize fear and risk, Marilyn needed to work toward Diving In to new territory with her clients. While she recognized this was scary for her, she could also see the possibilities. Her own life was fraught with this vacillation between choosing the "safe" idea and Diving In with something risky and new. She was enthusiastic about the possibility of mastering a new way of Diving In so that she and her clients could stop being stuck in the process.

During the creativity retreat, I had Marilyn practice Diving In. I knew that the more she could do this in her art, the more confidence she would gain to do it in therapy. One moment was particularly memorable. She had been working on one canvas for the entire retreat, and after about ten hours of painting in two days, Marilyn announced that she couldn't stand hearing herself talk about how much she liked her painting. We had been sharing intermittently between silent stretches of work. Whenever she shared, I started to feel frustrated and stuck with her. All she seemed to want to do was bask in her love for her painting. She had decided what it represented: "Each of these flowers is a member of my family. It's delightful for me to honor each person and interact with them as I paint." She had taken care to find just the right color for each of the flowers. She had gone over and over the same petal shapes she had started with by shading and adding subtle detail. She had been very successful in keeping her actions on the comfortable side.

In contrast, other participants were engaging in riskier acts in their paintings. One woman "jailed" her luminous moon with parallel black bars that covered her canvas. Another used white to cover everything except that which she enclosed with circles of various sizes. While the others were grappling with their processes on a deeper emotional level, Marilyn had been able to maintain status quo. I wanted her to have another go at Diving In. I knew she could engage initially and establish a sense of connection with both her painting and her clients, but once that happened, she needed to be able to Dive In with new ideas. That required Marilyn to practice taking risks.

I asked her, "What is one risky thing that you could do to your painting?"

She looked down to the ground thoughtfully, retrieved her Initial Idea, and then looked up at me with wide eyes. "I could make the flowers into clowns. But I don't know how to paint a clown. And I don't know how I'll like it."

I put my hand on her shoulder and gently invited her to Dive In—to paint the clowns however they showed up, and to honor her idea.

Several hours later, Marilyn's painting was transformed. She had added a few clown faces that hovered by the flowers in a bright landscape. It was whimsical, imaginative, and uniquely hers. She loved it. She loved the experience. She had found the courage to take a risk and as a result embraced a new way of Diving In. That day, as she left my office, she looked lighter and springier in her step.

As Marilyn's risk muscle got stronger in her art and her life, she was also able to apply it to her work in therapy. She developed a greater ease when it came to truth telling and confrontation in sessions with clients. "Now I get why my client's mom felt he needed to see another therapist," she realized. "He wasn't making progress. I wasn't challenging him, even when I wanted to. And he needed that." She was able to bring a variety of Initial Ideas into session, not just the ones that were "nice." As a result, she found a greater freedom and authenticity in how she interacted with clients, and recognized this act as a part of setting herself and her clients free from the status quo.

The Importance of Diving In

When we put our Initial Ideas to work, we are Diving In. Our creative process can't proceed without some kind of implementation. In many instances, as Marilyn discovered, our Initial Ideas feel different or uncomfortable. Our endeavors to cross-pollinate, see things from a variety of different perspectives, and even collaborate with our clients invite Initial Ideas that are brand new. Often Initial Ideas are so new that they bring a sense of uncertainty along with them. This can feel scary. We don't know what is going to happen when we use them in our third stage of the creative process. Even so, we need to be able to have the courage to risk not knowing how our art will turn out or how our client will respond, and Dive In to the process nonetheless.

We discover, like Marilyn did, that when we hold anxiety and excitement together in our work, we can feel a sense of vibrancy and authenticity. We enter new territory rich with meaning and value. And, very importantly, we are able to initiate the process of change by guiding our clients to these new places.

What Diving In Requires

- Befriending fear and anxiety
- Courage to risk
- Play.

Befriending Fear and Anxiety

We have already learned the importance of finding the "perfect danger" in an Initial Idea (Chapter 4). But thinking a "dangerous" thought is one thing; acting on it is another. Keeril Makan of the Kronos Quartet gives us an example of how he uses his experience of fear as a way to propel his creative process:

> *If while composing I become afraid of the music I am writing, I know that I have arrived at the extreme place where I want to be. When fear arises, I've reached the threshold between the known and the unknown. If I'm able to continue composing while tolerating the fear, I will be writing music that is new to me.*
>
> *(Makan, 2013)*

Makan doesn't back away from fear; instead, he uses it as a signal that he is composing something new. Fear, for Makan, is a good thing. If he can tolerate it, he is successfully able to navigate Diving In and immerse himself in the creative process without getting stuck.

Our fear in a therapy session might not be as intense as Makan's fear of the music he is writing. Nevertheless, it is natural to experience anxiety or nervousness when taking a risk with a client. Like Marilyn, we might be inclined to believe that this anxiety is a sign that we're in dangerous territory and decide to back away onto safer ground. But we can choose, as Makan does, to see our anxiety as a signal that we are up to something good. The therapists in Orlinsky and Rønnestad's (2005) research know this well. As I mentioned in the Introduction to this book, they reported having experienced both Anxiety and Flow in the same session the majority of the time. They didn't let anxiety or fear block them from successfully navigating the creative process and getting to the fifth stage, Flow.

Courage to Risk

I asked a group of therapists, "What is the riskiest thing you've done in your life and how has it affected your creativity?" Their stories were inspiring. Some moved out of the country; others quit a job and went back to school; another adopted a child late in life. No matter the risk, the process was the same. Each and every risk required a great amount of courage in order for the therapists to literally Dive In to a new phase in their lives. Invariably they felt propelled, energized, and highly creative as a result. Some of the risks resulted in failure or a dead end, but even those therapists could see that this "mistake" was vital for figuring out the next step and staying creative.

The therapist group's risk stories generated intense discussion about the role of safety and risk in our lives. The group decided that all too often they had tried to mitigate risk in their lives and in their work. They'd all had powerful experiences of risk spurring creativity, and yet they each recognized times in their lives when they had become bored and uninspired because of the routine and structure they had established.

During a lecture in 2015, Irvin Yalom mentioned that during first sessions with each patient, he asks them to agree to take at least one risk in each session. This was interesting to me in light of what I knew about the role of risk in the creative process. I took a risk of my own and called him up to ask more. In our conversation, Dr. Yalom told me that he invites his patient to take a risk if the therapy has stalled or he senses that they aren't getting anywhere. He will, in essence, ask his patient to Dive In further and talk about what isn't being said. When he invites this risk, he is inviting the patient to gather courage and propel the session forward. He asks his patient to practice taking risks as a way of enlivening the work and deepening the therapeutic relationship. Indeed, he and his patients navigate the Diving In stage session after session.

How is it that we can know how enlivening risks can be and yet still choose not to Dive In? Unfortunately, risk is too often paired with fear of making mistakes. I'm so grateful to have learned from Scott Miller that this error-phobic stance is in fact an invitation to mediocrity (as I discuss in the Introduction). We strive to gain a sense of confidence by learning a set of clinical protocols or theoretical approach, and in doing so we gain a sense of proficiency. Then, like Marilyn, because we feel comfortable, we repeat the same things over and over again. We tend not to take risks to find unique ways to approach each client.

In Diving In with a risky Initial Idea for her flower painting, Marilyn recognized that she had been keeping herself shielded from the fear of making mistakes by keeping her painting safe. In confronting her fear, she found that it was more valuable to risk painting clowns that didn't make sense than to endlessly retrace her flower petals. She recognized that this risk taking was essential to moving her clinical work beyond rapport building and into change.

Marilyn learned to listen to her "weird" ideas and to allow them more time and consideration. Rather than immediately eliminating them, she consciously explored ones that had some risk attached to them. For instance, she had always made it a practice to teach each client some form of mindfulness practice. With her stronger risk muscle, she came up with interesting new ways in which she could talk about mindfulness. She even used her risk muscle to talk to clients about how they could bring risk into their own lives. Marilyn's response to risk taking turned out to be more inspiring and life affirming than she had ever thought it would be. With her newfound courage, she was able to Dive In despite the risks and teach her clients to do the same.

Play

There's a delightful YouTube video depicting a young boy in the doctor's office about to have his vaccinations. His doctor is brilliantly using tissues to perform magic tricks and make the child giggle. The fun that the two are having is palpable. The doctor gives the boy his first shot while cascades of tissue rain down between the two of them. The boy laughs and doesn't even seem to notice the injection. The second shot is accompanied by more giggles in response to the doctor's sustained sense of fun and play with the tissues.

This video is a wonderful example of how play and fun alleviate our fear response. Many therapists I work with end up deciding that they are way too serious with clients. They realize that the high expectations they place on themselves to be good at what they do often fosters a somber approach that is antithetical to creativity. Play invites us to shift our focus. When we bring a sense of humor or playfulness to anxiety-provoking situations, our bodies relax and our experiences transform. And when we embrace a sense of play and humor as an ally in Diving In, we are less likely to freeze in response to our fears in session.

Finding Sponge Bob

The feather earrings and Doc Marten lace-ups were my first clue about the type of therapist Mandy was. As she picked her seat for the training I was giving that day in her hometown, I thought, *I bet she's an awesome teen therapist.* I watched her colorful macramé bracelets move up and down her arm as she took notes and raised her hand to ask excellent questions. Most of us don't think we can get away with dressing and being exactly who we are, but it appeared that Mandy did this with grace.

I had the privilege of continuing to work with Mandy through my online workshop, Artfix. She was brave in her exploration of her own creative process, and I got to witness the incredible effort she put into mastering Diving In.

I had been right in my first impression of Mandy. For the first 18 years of her career, she had worked at a wilderness school for troubled teens. She described her work with young people and families as "alternative." She wasn't taught theory or specific techniques; instead, she and the program emphasized the relationship between teen and adult as the primary catalyst for change. She worked to accept that she couldn't control things in the relationship. She leaned on her ability to be present with her clients and to think unconventionally to inspire new ways of thinking and being, often using their natural surroundings as metaphors for what was happening in the moment.

When I met Mandy, she was no longer working at the wilderness school but had become the lead therapist for a juvenile detention center. The environment was, needless to say, in marked contrast to the wilderness experience she was used to. The detention center's formalized treatment standard dictated much of what could happen in session with her clients. Mandy struggled to fit into the standard and often felt stifled by the rules. Here, in her current job, she had started to question herself. She grappled with her image, wanting to know whether she should look and sound like other therapists. When she tried to "work within the lens of others," she said, she just fell on her butt. Her fears about not being good enough were diminishing her excitement and confidence in her work.

In her Creative Process Assessment (Chapter 2), Mandy identified that she was most often blocked in her Diving In Stage. That is, her self-doubts around her "outside the box" way of working often stopped her from doing what she really wanted to do in therapy. Her ability to come up with Initial Ideas was well developed, and from her experience at the wilderness center she knew how to identify the ones with the "perfect danger." But now, at the detention center, she experienced a block to Diving In during a session, discarding a spontaneous idea that she hadn't tried before even when her instinct told her it would be great. The times that she didn't throw the idea away but implemented it instead, she had wonderful "aha" moments with her clients.

One such moment was particularly memorable for Mandy. Her 16-year-old client, Nellie, had lived on the streets and prostituted herself to survive. The trauma that Nellie had weathered was horrifying. Her scars from self-harm created two sleeves of white-and-pink lines. That day, Mandy remembered feeling particularly sensitive to Nellie's dysregulated state. Mandy was looking for a way to teach self-compassion to Nellie but their dialogue felt superficial. An idea popped into Mandy's imaginative mind: *I want her to put Band-Aids on her scars.* Mandy decided to act on her thought, and despite the unconventional approach and the risk that Nellie would reject the idea (and perhaps Mandy), she shared it with Nellie. She told Nellie that she felt like giving her scars Band-Aids because "even though the cuts have healed, you have not." In response, Nellie asked in a very young voice, "Do you have any Band-Aids with Sponge Bob on them?"

They both laughed at this question and decided to draw their own pictures onto the plain Band-Aids that were available. For the rest of the session, Mandy and Nellie drew hearts and flowers and butterflies and one Sponge Bob. Each time a Band-Aid was finished, Mandy would invite Nellie to put it on while they named the healing power it contained. "This Band-Aid is full of love. This Band-Aid shall give me freedom. This Band-Aid reminds me to play." It was a magical intervention, made even more magical by Mandy's ability to Dive In with her very own approach to her client's unique set of issues.

At the end of our online course, Mandy told the group, "I realized that every time I have an aha moment with a client, I've been present with myself and okay with whatever crazy idea came up. It's all about laughter, giggles, accepting, and taking the risk." Mandy had learned that she needed to embrace a part of herself that she hadn't allowed into session before. Even though this sometimes went against the expectations of her organization, she allowed herself to navigate her creative process with clients in this way. In the end, she decided that she did better work and her clients benefited even more.

How to Get Better at Diving In

Cultivate Child-like Wonder

I cherish a vivid memory from a summer birthday party in my adolescence. The piñata hung from a pine limb as my family and friends stood in a semi-circle laughing, clapping, and enjoying the anticipation as my cousin Ashley wielded the bat. We were mesmerized by the paper donkey's swing, and then the whack, and the prizes that began to rain down onto to the soft pine-needle floor. Time slowed and, as if magnetized, our eyes locked onto two-year-old Ben, who had spotted a shiny blue ball amidst the candy and confetti. He stepped in, arms outstretched, and toddled toward the ball. He was in love with his discovery and we were all in love with his wonder. For that instant, we saw what he saw, and we melted with the innocence and beauty as we collectively hushed and looked through the eyes of a child.

We were all so hypnotized that we didn't remember to tell Ashley that she had cracked the piñata. She took another swing only to make contact with poor Ben and his new ball. When the paddle made contact with his face, I was jarred out of that wonder and back into a world of fear and worry and pain. We all burst into action and let the magical moment go. Ben suffered a sore mouth and jaw, but was just fine in the end. That night, I watched his sister give him the ball that he had dropped after he'd been hit. He hugged it close as if to squeeze some of its magic into his heart.

It is rare that we get to see with the raw innocence that a child does. As adults, we use our prior experiences as a lens and end up comparing and contrasting rather than simply being present. While there is a time and place for calling upon prior experience, Diving In with a client is not one of those times.

When we cultivate a beginner's spirit, we surrender to uncertainty. We can't know what will happen when we see from this new lens; we must yield to not-knowing and still proceed. This brings a fresh, unique perspective to the therapeutic process and fuels our creative endeavor. When we Dive In with a client, we must be willing to surrender. Musician, composer, and author Stephen Nachmanovitch (1990: p.21), in describing this state of letting go, writes, "Surrender means cultivating a comfortable attitude toward not-knowing, being nurtured by the mystery of moments that are dependably surprising, ever fresh." We must let go of an old way of seeing in order to usher in the new and fresh surprise. Once we take that first step of action with a client, it becomes not so much about the doing, but being present to the process, watching what unfolds. Whether it's the first time or the thousandth time you've invited a client to draw a mandala or change a negative belief or whatever your Initial Idea tells you to do, you need to see the response as if it's never been done before. This moment is brand new, and you and the client are here to create it together.

Mandy talked about watching a client cry from this new perspective. "Those tears were the most beautiful things," she told me. "I was so in the moment with my client that I wasn't thinking about what to do for her; instead, I was just captured by the way her tears rolled down her cheeks. I watched and stayed utterly present because it was such a new experience."

Practice Letting Go

On my first rafting trip, I learned an important lesson about letting go from my Grampa Bill. That summer, he had taken all of the grandkids on a multi-day adventure down the Tuolumne River. I was both scared and exhilarated by the white water as we splashed our way down one tricky rapid after another. Our guide was an expert at navigating these rapids and would call out commands like, "Hard right!" or "Back paddle, back paddle, hard, hard!" I was anxious after hearing stories about boats overturning or getting stuck on rocks or in eddies. So I followed the guide's directions and responded to his callouts with conviction and energy and lots and lots of muscle.

There was one particular rapid, ominously named Hell's Kitchen, where we had to bounce off of one rock in order to miss a bigger one. I was terrified that we wouldn't get it right and would end up overturned in the most treacherous part of the river. As we set course into the rapid, my lips were white and my hands shook. We had to paddle directly toward a rock, which felt wrong and totally dangerous. The guide shouted, "Harder, harder!" As I dug in with my paddle, I caught a glimpse of Grampa Bill on the other side of the boat. He wasn't paddling at all. He was just smiling blissfully. He looked as if he was sitting at home in front of the fireplace. I yelled to him, "Paddle, Grampa Bill, paddle!" He just waved.

When we reached calm water and I could breathe again, I asked my grandfather, "Why didn't you paddle?" I was slightly irritated that he hadn't followed the guide's instructions, and perplexed because he was so strong and physical. It just didn't make sense. He said, "I want to feel the power of the water. If I'm busy paddling and worrying about where we're going, I can't let go and enjoy the ride."

I admire my Grampa Bill for his ability to let go on the river. What he taught me has stuck as a valuable lesson to apply to the creative process and Diving In.

When we work as therapists, we set a course by taking action on our Initial Idea. When we introduce a topic, invite our client to express a feeling, or employ any kind of technique or clinical protocol, we start our descent into the rapid. If we white-knuckle it, we will be rigid and insecure. We will be working so hard that we miss important subtleties along the way. In the end, we may arrive with our client at the intended destination—point taken, insight made, changes committed to. But we will never know what we missed by trying so hard.

Those beautiful moments of surprise when we can't believe the power of therapy, when we and our client feel the palpable presence of change that feeds hope, are made by letting go and enjoying the ride. We have to invite ourselves to take the pressure off and see where the process will take us. Whenever I feel my body tense like I'm about to tackle white water, I think of my Grampa Bill perched serenely on his side of the boat "feeling the power of the water and loving it."

Follow the Energy

It was the end of a long day. Feeling tired and a bit hungry, I was craving the fold of my family at the dinner table and our evening routine. My last client, Sean, was due any second. I knew he'd come barreling in, after-school snack half-eaten, asking, "What are we gonna do today?" I was carefully weighing my energy level against the session plan that I had come up with earlier in the day.

That morning, I had been energized from my river walk and calmed from my yoga stretches. The day had seemed imminently doable. I had been hit with what felt like a huge "aha" idea that could address the anticipatory anxiety that caused Sean to resist trying anything new. Of course, at the time, the use of paper towel rolls, large spans of cardboard, and lots and lots of glue-gun glue seemed like fun, engaging, sink-your-teeth-in creativity. Now, it just seemed like a lot of work. I was afraid of what it would require of me. Diving In with little Sean this afternoon seemed a bit treacherous, like I could get swallowed up in the process, and I felt I didn't have the energy to carry that kind of session.

But since I had been working so consciously to partner with my creativity, in that decisive moment, I dared myself to Dive In. I reminded myself how energizing a creative risk can be, even when I'm exhausted, and I remembered sessions when I had stood on the edge of that cliff, never quite leaping, and at the end, wishing I had because we just didn't get as far as we could have. I had come to identify my feeling of rigidity as an indication that something new was about to happen. That great question posed itself: "If I treated this session as my art and set off with my client to create a masterpiece (no product necessary—just the act of collaborating), would I Dive In with all of the energy I could muster?"

And, in the name of creativity, I rallied. I suggested the idea of making a bridge and gave Sean a large piece of cardboard. He loved the idea and added his own creative touches. We spent 45 minutes gluing paper towel rolls along the edge to make a guardrail. He drew stop signs and danger exclamations on the entry side to represent his fear. I found some old New Year's Eve poppers to put on the other side to indicate the excitement that he often experienced once he managed his anxiety and accomplished the task that he'd been avoiding.

By the end of that 45 minutes, we had a full-scale highway on-ramp. Not a two-dimensional, try-to-imagine-it kind of ramp. Not a walk-your-fingers-across-and-pretend kind of ramp. We had built a *whole ramp* that we could walk on and over and through. We practiced coming up to the entry and experiencing the danger signals. He named them: "People are going to think I'm weird. I'm not going to be good enough. I won't be able to get ahold of my mom so she can pick me up." From where he stood, he could see and name the poppers and glitter on the other side. We dipped his feet in paint and had him make footprints walking in the direction of the celebration. He walked, I cheered, he gleamed. The insights and kinesthetic learning were remarkable. Rather than feeling drained and inefficient, as I had dreaded, Sean and I were both energized.

When I went home that night, I didn't slump at the dinner table. I was happy and fulfilled, and grateful in knowing I had a job where I could be helpful and richly creative all at the same time.

The experience that Sean and I had reminded me again of the lesson that my Grampa Bill taught me on the river: sometimes you have to let go in order to enjoy the ride.

Diving In with Clients

It was the second Thursday evening in a row I had found myself wrapped in a stifling blanket of doubt. I left the intensity of my engagement with the family I was working with and joined my observer-self in the corner where the ceiling met the walls. *Shoot, now what? You really can't help these people,* I mumbled inside my head. I began clicking through potential referrals—people or programs that might be more adept, more intense, more whatever it was that I didn't have.

The emotional tension inside threatened to break—the silent implosion that signaled resignation, disappointment, failure. I wondered what I could come up with besides a sloppily delivered confrontation that carried unfair blame or judgment. I wondered if there was anything I could actually do that would be helpful.

I had been listening to my teen client's two moms matter-of-factly list the worrisome infractions that their daughter had committed during the last week. She had snuck out, locked herself in the bathroom, stormed out of the house, refused to talk. They had removed her bedroom door, taken away her phone, and put her under "house arrest." She was sitting in my office, arms crossed, lips zipped into a tight white line while tears streaked down her cheeks. As her mothers ran down their list, they missed seeing their daughter's tears falling to the table.

It was that place again, that nearly intolerable cesspool, the place where so many questions swarmed without answers and I wondered if I would ever come up for air. I was just like Marilyn in this place. I knew what I needed to do. I had my Initial Idea. I had come up with it prior to even hearing them talk about the week. But I was scared to death that I couldn't pull it off. I knew I needed to tell these parents hard truths, and it broke my heart to think that when I did they would either cry in agony or leave in a rage. I wanted to stay in the comfort of rapport building by empathizing with their disappointment over their teen's wrongdoings, but I was certain that remaining comfortable wasn't the answer. I was absolutely *uncertain* as to how to Dive In and tell them that their approach to parenting was a bigger problem than their teen's behavior.

And, yet, somewhere faintly in the background, I remembered last Thursday's drive home, smiling and goosefleshed— side effects of the therapist's high I was experiencing. I hadn't broken under the tension in that session with a different family. I had let it simmer, and just prior to boiling, my words poured out on a wave of compassion and risk. I Dived In and spoke the absolute truth, gently, resolutely. At first, I had to hold my ground despite my shaking feet. And then, my clients came along, stepping into a new perspective. Eyes open, heads tilted, they saw with me the truth that needed so desperately to be changed. The shift happened in all of us. The tension was gone, and clarity's vision brought relief and excitement for what was to come.

I knew what I had to do in this session: I had to confront these parents on their punitive stance with their teen. But I didn't have the answer about *how* best to do this. I was convinced that the solution was beyond my reach and that I wasn't going to get anywhere with these clients. So, on this chilly Thursday evening, knowing my creative process and how easily doubt can shut me down, I tolerated the churning and cast aside the blanket of doubt. I walked to the edge of caution and decided to jump. I told these parents what was so troubling to me about their situation.

"If you were to shift and think about the most important thing—your relationship with your daughter—what would you be saying or doing differently?" I asked them. I reworded it several times and allowed my emotion to show. Finally, they saw it. They saw that they'd been focusing on their daughter's misbehavior and, in the process, destroying their relationships with her. They got it, and wanted to know what they could do to change. I was relieved, again, as I had been with the other family. I reached into my skills/techniques pocket and offered them three concrete actions that I knew would help, all the while doing a happy dance inside my head.

Having taken the risk, having tolerated the uncertainty, I had Dived In. As a result, my clients were committed to making concrete changes that would help their entire family. And I got to drive home feeling that therapist's high—the adrenaline rush that comes from experiencing a moment of Flow after surrendering to uncertainty.

Diving In requires courage. It's a lesson I have to remind myself of constantly. When I feel the fear, it means that something new is about to happen. I need to take the risk and let go of needing to feel certain.

Summary

The third stage of the creative process, Diving In, is a stage of action. It marks a transition from thinking to doing. In order to navigate this third stage, we need to have strong risk muscles. We need to muster the courage necessary to go with our clients into the unknown. Sometimes it is scary; others times it is exhilarating. Whatever the emotion associated with risk, we can learn to treat it as an invitation to Dive In. Because play, humor, and child-like wonder spawn relaxation and exhilaration, they are wonderful elements to welcome into this stage.

Successfully Diving In means not letting our fear of making a mistake stop us from using our Initial Ideas. In art, when we Dive In, we are creating. In therapy, when we Dive In, we are engaging and asking our clients to risk. We Dive In despite potential mistakes or reactions, and we arrive at the fourth stage, Flexible Commitment, poised to refine, collaborate, and continue our creative process.

Questions to Ponder

1. How do you respond to spontaneous ideas that occur to you about a client, either during or outside of session?
2. Do you experience the self-doubt and self-censorship that Mandy struggled with? How does it affect you? How does it affect your work?
3. Does comfort with the status quo keep you from taking risks in session?
4. Does your wish to be seen as kind, empathetic, and compassionate prevent you from Diving In with your client?
5. How do most of your sessions feel? How do you want them to feel?
6. How might you change your way of being in session to get to the feeling you wish for?
7. Can you cultivate a child-like wonder about one of your clients? What new thoughts or perspectives arise?
8. Do you bring a sense of play or humor into your sessions? What does that do for your creative process and your therapeutic process?
9. Name a risk that you've taken in your life. How has it affected your creativity?

Art Invitations

What Blocks You?

This art activity is designed to help you see what can prevent you from Diving In and, in addition, identify resources that are useful in keeping you from getting stuck in this stage of the creative process. The blocks can be caused for a variety of reasons and are very personalized. It is helpful to make art about these blocks or "triggers" and the way you cope with them so that you can recover quickly when they happen.

Here's what you need:

- Journal or scratch paper
- Drawing paper (11″ x 14″ or bigger)
- Magazine images
- Scissors
- Glue stick.

Here's how:

1. Free-write responses to these prompts in your journal or on scratch paper:
   - In therapy, what I fear most is . . .
   - I freeze when my client . . .
   - The hardest thing for me in doing therapy is . . .
2. Identify a theme in your list. For instance, you might notice a theme of fear of making mistakes or unrealistic expectations. We will define this theme as your "trigger."
3. Fold your large piece of drawing paper in half. On the top half of your paper, paste magazine images that relate to your chosen theme. Try to find images that capture the emotional tone of your theme.
4. Now free-write responses to these prompts:
   - The thing that relaxes me every time is . . .
   - I relax when I think about . . .
   - The thing I love about doing therapy is . . .
5. Consider your responses to the above prompts and formulate an idea about what helps you move beyond the trigger and let go. For instance, you might choose breathing or present-moment awareness.
4. On the bottom half of your paper, paste magazine images that relate to your chosen theme. Try to find images that capture that which soothes your "trigger."
5. Now take a look at your paper and see how the two halves relate. Are there opposites? Are there similarities? What do

your images tell you about your trigger and how to cope with it in session?

Note: The examples pictured are a more complex form of creating a "pop-up." If you are interested in making this, you can find the template in the Resources section at the back of the book. There is also a helpful video that walks you through the activity at www.innercanvas.com/creativity-cotherapist.

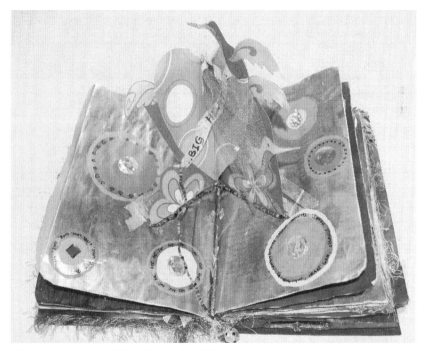

Figure 5.1 Susan's "What Blocks You?"

Susan worked with her trigger in an altered book. She said, "The pop-up represents how I'm triggered by clients who never get angry or assertive. I'm thinking of someone who is all heart and loves everybody, who sees everything through rose-colored glasses." She recognized how much this reaction makes it difficult for her to Dive In with a client. She realized that seeing her client in a broader perspective was a necessary part of being able to identify her other relevant qualities and aspects. "The background represents this with gems and many more colors. It reminds me to look beyond the trigger so I don't get stuck and blocked."

Figure 5.2 Belinda's "What Blocks You?"

Belinda's trigger looks like a big V. She said, "This V stands for Victim. While I have a lot of compassion for clients, when they seem stuck on blaming everything in their past, I tend to get very stuck." Belinda depicted herself as a stone bust behind bars because of the reaction she has to clients who initially present in this way. She added outdoor images and softened the look with fluffy yarn. She realized, "If I want to Dive In with someone who feels powerless because of their past, I can't be cold and stony. I have to embody something more expansive and soft. This will be helpful to me if I feel myself going there."

Holding On and Letting Go

When you can visually represent physical sensations or states of being, the experiences of these states become vivid and more accessible. The idea for this art activity is to be able to identify your state of holding on and to invite yourself to let go—a crucial skill in Diving In.

Here's what you need:

- Drawing paper (two sheets)
- Oil pastels or chalk pastels.

Here's how:

1. Tense up your body. Pretend that you are clutching something with your hands. Clench your jaw. Put yourself in a state of holding on. Pay attention to the feelings and sensations.
2. On your piece of paper draw the words "Holding On" with the same feelings and sensations that you experienced in Step 1. If you like, you can draw the words over and over again in different iterations of the same state of tension.
3. Relax your body. Take deep breaths and sink into your seat. Soften your jaw. Put yourself in a state of letting go. Pay attention to the feelings and sensations.
4. Get a different piece of paper and draw the words "Letting Go" with the same feelings and sensations you experienced in step 3. If you like, you can draw the words over and over again in different iterations of the same state of letting go.
5. Look at your drawings. As you gaze at each one, can you feel the state in your body? Are there particular elements in your drawings that capture each state more intensely than other elements?
6. Practice visualizing your picture of holding on while you tense your body. Then practice visualizing your picture of letting go while you experience your body relaxing.
7. When in session, try to access your image of letting go and the relaxed feeling you captured while drawing it. Notice how this can help you shift when you are attempting to Dive In but experiencing fear or anxiety.

Figure 5.3 Carol's "Holding On"

Holding On for Carol felt scary. She felt there was pressure and smallness. Her tree is tiny against the vast landscape, and yet it is all very controlled. She related these feelings to the sensation of holding her breath. She said, "Sometimes I feel this way with a client when I don't know how things are going to turn out."

Figure 5.4 Carol's "Letting Go"

Letting Go for Carol was very different from her first painting. She said she envisioned a tall cliff with water flowing over it. It felt scary to imagine the cliff in her painting, but once she started to paint the water, it "felt really deep and beautiful. And then the excitement came. I felt like celebrating! I did it!" She talked about the courage that it took for her to just let go and how much of a relief it was. She wants to remember this painting for times when she has that Holding On sensation in session. "If I can remember the excitement that comes with letting go, I will be so much better off, and I know my client will be, too."

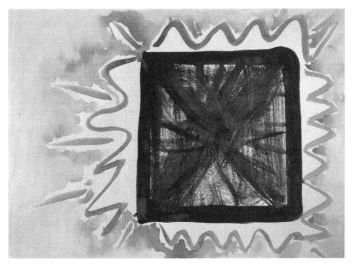

Figure 5.5 Jamie's "Holding On" (see color version in plate section)

For Jamie, Holding On felt contained, dense, dark, pressured, and full of longing. She became aware of how much energy it takes for her to "hold on." She could also see how "holding on" keeps her from seeing outside the box. She said, "If I take a risk and stop holding on so tightly, I can see the light and beauty that is on the outside."

Figure 5.6 Jamie's "Letting Go" (see color version in plate section)

When Jamie painted "Letting Go," she felt tears coming at the beginning. "Instead of a dense, dark feeling in my chest, it feels like it's opening and expansive and playful and free." Instead of fearful, she felt curious and inquisitive. She said, "If I can hold this experience and use it, it could inform so much of my work."

Honor Your Action Taker

Many therapists I know, including myself, attribute their ability to Dive In and take action to a specific aspect of themselves. Sometimes it is easier to call on a part of yourself that has these action capabilities than to tell yourself to just do it. But you need to get to know this part of you in order to be able to utilize it when you need to.

Here's what you need:

- Magazine image
- Small frame (store-bought or homemade with paper).

Here's how:

1. Think of the last several times you have decided to implement something, such as following through on a decision, speaking up about something you have needed to address, starting a project, talking about a particular direction you'd like to go with a client. Write a list of several examples that happened recently.
2. Review this list and, as you read your examples, visualize yourself doing them. What do you look like? How do you stand? What energy do you project? Really take stock of this part of you who takes action.
3. Now make a list of words that describe this part of you: upbeat, powerful, confident, graceful, elaborate, brave, untouchable, etc.
4. Find an image in a magazine or on the Internet that matches these words. Put this picture in a frame so that you can honor your action taker. Place the frame in an important spot so that you can remember that you have an action taker when you need to Dive In with a client.

Figure 5.7 Hannah's Action Taker

Hannah's action taker is a honey eater. She talked about her bird: "It's like she's doing bird yoga. She's sort of twisted, but she's poised for action at the same time. Her colors are quiet." Hannah identified the ways in which she sees her action taker operating on the job. "In the hospital setting, my action taker allows me to get into a lot of places that I couldn't otherwise because I'm camouflaged. I'm ready to go and do whatever it is I need to before anybody knows it." She reported a sense of clarity after having finished her art activity. In the process, she realized that her action taker moves so quickly that there are times when she wonders if she should be a little slower. Exploring the way her action taker works for her helped her understand that her way didn't have to match others' speeds.

Figure 5.8 Kristen's Action Taker

Kristen sees her action taker as a tree climber. She said, "I'm going up into something I'm not sure of, but I'm climbing in order to get the perspective that I need in order to be able to see for my clients." She was reminded of the time she spent onstage as an actor and the vulnerability that came with that experience. She felt immersed in acting, just like her tree climber is immersed in climbing. And yet, she noted, "Both are so exposed. We risk like that for the sake of our art. I can see how important it is to do that for our clients."

Figure 3.2 Jamie's "Drips"

Figure 3.4 Carol's "Rainbow Breathing"

Figure 3.6 Christine's "Where Does it Belong?"

Figure 4.1 Robin's "Follow the Rhythm Until it Changes"

Figure 4.5 Group's NOW! Watches

Figure 5.5 Jamie's "Holding On"

Figure 5.6 Jamie's "Letting Go"

Figure 6.2 Susan's "Happy Accident"

Figure 6.5 Jamie's "Stuck"

Figure 6.6 Jamie's "New Perspective"

Figure 6.7d Susan's Sustained Painting Stage 4

Figure 6.8d Shelley's Sustained Painting Stage 4

Figure 7.1 Gratitude Tags

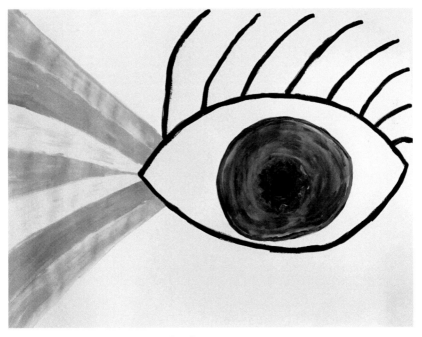

Figure 7.2 Carly's "Honoring Flow"

Figure 7.3 Ruth's "Honoring Flow"

Figure 8.4 A Page in Belinda's Book

6

FLEXIBLE COMMITMENT

Many of the therapists I have worked with experience a block in their creative process at the Flexible Commitment stage. Once we have taken the action to Dive In, Flexible Commitment asks us to master the art of simultaneously holding on to our commitment to the process and letting go of the exact outcome. To navigate this stage is to sustain a dual relationship to surrender and to discipline. An artist engaged in painting will inevitably experience rough patches where her creation doesn't proceed as planned. A therapist will likely encounter times of client resistance or inadvertently fail to empathize with her client. Despite these challenges, we have to proceed, holding our commitment to the process in the forefront of our minds. At the same time, we can't do this with force or rigidity. Stephen Nachmanovitch (1990: p. 189) describes the light touch with which we need to approach commitment at this stage of the creative process: "Creativity always involves a certain amount of discipline, self-restraint, and self-sacrifice." However, he explains, "The creative surprise often takes place when the pressure comes off in an episode of relaxation or surrender" (Nachmanovitch, 1990: p. 154). The ability to engage in the back and forth dialogue between discipline and surrender are vital to navigating the Flexible Commitment stage.

When I was in graduate school, my beloved professor Susan Orr, an art therapist and meditation instructor, made sure we heard this message loud and clear. She came to class one day wielding a handful of fanned-out strips of paper. With a mischievous look, she offered her hand to each one of us. When it came time for me to choose a strip of paper, I felt like I was selecting a special prophecy from this wise woman—something that would provide earth-shattering revelation for years to come, something that was divined for me and me alone.

It turned out we all got the same message. It said, "Try trusting the Art." I thought I understood what she was trying to say at the time, but it wasn't until a good decade later that I could actually embody that trust. I have the strip of paper she made on a dot matrix printer some 30 years ago taped to my desktop. It reminds me that the creative process and the therapeutic process are just that—processes. When we encounter impasses, make mistakes, or lose the thread, we can trust that these are as much a part of the process as any other experience. By trusting this, we can stay committed to the process without giving up or getting blocked.

To understand Flexible Commitment further, it might be helpful to imagine an artist at her easel. Let's say she's engaged in the act of painting, which means she has gone through her Incubating stage and been able to come up with an Initial Idea. She has begun to take action on her Initial Idea by starting to put colors on the canvas. Any anxiety she had at the start has yielded to excitement because she's curious about creating something new. And then, inevitably, she encounters a moment: she's slightly disoriented because she feels she might have lost her way. She took the plunge into her creative act, but is now unsure of where it will lead. It's a terrifying moment to look up from her canvas and realize that she is midway, without directional bearings. She can't go back to the blank white and yet she can't see the end product.

Here, our artist has come to the stage of Flexible Commitment, another place where creative possibilities flood in. It is the place of improvisation. She has to let go of the exact outcome and give up how it "should" be done. If she can continue to trust her process and, in so doing, stay committed to her painting, gradually her art crosses the divide from old to new. She might need to revisit her second stage and bring in a new Initial Idea. This will invite her to Dive In all over again. She may do this many times over the course of her painting. Each time she does this, she has successfully navigated the fourth stage of the creative process, Flexible Commitment, and will likely celebrate a moment of Flow.

In the stories and case studies that follow, we will see how the fourth stage of the creative process, Flexible Commitment, invites us to go back through the previous stages of the process. Flexible Commitment can be a crossroads of sorts where the choice is between "trusting the art" and becoming blocked.

Window Exit

"I want to burn them," she mumbled, eyes locked on the mound of torn paper she had made from her painting.

"All right," I nodded, "but we can't burn stuff in the office. It will set off the smoke alarm."

Her eyes rolled. "Fine, then let's do it outside."

I did a quick mental check about confidentiality, fire hazards, and general trauma treatment, and decided to go with the idea. Brandy was a challenging 15-year-old client who pushed my limits. Her grandmother had brought her to therapy after getting custody at the end of a long battle with Child Protective Services. Brandy's mom hadn't been able to provide for her daughter for many years, but had always managed to pull things together just enough to keep Brandy at home. Finally, the school had stepped in, and in order to prevent Brandy from being expelled due to her aggressive and conflict-laden interactions with peers, her mom had sent her to live with her grandmother. Brandy didn't hold anything back. She was angry, uncooperative, and a general bully. She smoked pot in the school bathroom, got into fistfights after school, and refused to do homework. She also loved art and wanted someone to love her.

I often found myself at a decision point in sessions with her. She had a sense of outrageousness that I admired, but sometimes it knocked me outside of my comfort zone. It wasn't uncommon for me to invite her into an art activity and for her to take my idea to extremes—bigger paper, louder music than I wanted. The time I suggested she work silently, she didn't talk for two sessions.

The day she wanted to burn her art, I had thought that her work during the session was powerful and complete. That day, we had started talking about an argument she'd had with her grandmother on the drive over to my office, which had then led to her sharing how powerless she felt in her life and how unfair it always seemed. I had invited her to paint an expression of her powerlessness and knew that the very act of representing this experience would help her connect with an internal sense of power.

Sure enough, her painting began as a small black dot in the middle of the page. It grew and grew into an intense jumble of red and black brush strokes that covered the entire 24-by-36-inch piece of paper. At various points, I narrated Brandy's painting: "Now you are adding more red splatters." "The black drips are going all the way down the page." And she responded to me, "This is how angry I am." "This is how awful it made me feel." When she placed the last brush in the water container, she stepped back and looked with wide eyes.

"You had a lot to say about powerlessness!" I said passionately.

"It's about abuse. My abuse, you know, from my mom. I'm titling it 'Abuse.'" And that's when she ripped it into tiny pieces.

She cried. I witnessed.

She collected the pieces that had fallen to the floor and made a mound. I told her that the whole process was beautiful. She thanked me. I thought we were finished. She had done an amazing job of addressing her powerlessness and trauma. She had expressed and transformed the way in which she held the experience. I knew there would be more to come, but for today, I thought we had done well. That was when Brandy said, "I want to burn them." That was a decision point for me, and, I decided to keep going with her.

I peered through the window that looked out onto the back deck and didn't see anyone around. I grabbed a ceramic bowl and some matches and suggested to Brandy that she bring her pile of painting pieces and head out to the deck with me. I started toward the office door to exit, but Brandy didn't move. "No way!" she said loudly. "I'm not going out there! We'd have to pass my grandmother in the waiting room. I don't want to see her, especially with this!" She held up the mound of red and black painted papers cupped in her hand.

Brandy eyed the window. It led to the wraparound deck and was only a few feet above the deck floor. "Let's climb out the window," she said. She put the papers down on the table and headed to lift the sash.

Here we go again, I thought, and I felt myself go rigid. *If she's not going to cooperate, then we just aren't going to do this burning idea at all. I gave her a choice, and she's just pushing the limits more.* I started to say, "No." But before I could get it out, I saw the childlike grin on Brandy's face. Her look wasn't one of malice or defiance. She was looking at me so sweetly. "I can teach you this," she said. "I climb out windows all the time. It's so much fun. Just try it with me? Please?"

I relaxed. I smiled. I felt myself become pliable. And I helped her move the paintbrush tins from the windowsill.

She went first, crouching to get through the small opening. I handed her the bowl and the papers. Then she held out her hand to help me through the open window. We arrived together on the deck, giggling at our secret getaway. The mood had changed. She was no longer the traumatized teen with a chip on her shoulder and I was no longer the rule-keeping authority figure.

She lit the pieces of paper and we watched as, one by one, they turned the white ceramic bowl grey with ash. The process was complete for the day. We climbed back through the window satiated.

As she left my office, she asked, "Next week I want to use the ashes to paint a window, okay?"

Climbing through the window with Brandy that day was liberating for both of us. I was able to let go of an agenda about the exact outcome of Brandy's art. Brandy was able to follow her creative process and find more resolution with her expression of pain. She was able to do this in a unique way without having to defy me. That day, we collaborated and shaped the session together. Her insistence on climbing out the window had brought me right up to a place inside where I had to make a choice. I could have said no. I'm glad I didn't, because if I had, I would have blocked both Brandy and myself in the creative process and likely (at least for that day) in the therapeutic process.

There was another time similar to the window exit session. I had pushed Brandy beyond where she wanted to go with one too many questions about her volatile relationship with her siblings. She was the youngest and felt defenseless when her older siblings fought. She always ended up in the line of fire. I had been trying to understand the dynamic so I could help her feel safer. The topic alone rendered her defenseless, and I'm certain she experienced my questions as just adding to the pile. In her infinite wisdom, 15 minutes into our session, after that one question too many, she got up and left. She walked right past her grandmother in the waiting room and down the street.

I didn't know what to do, but I knew that I wasn't going to just let her end the session. I felt committed and obligated to see where this was going to go. I walked into the waiting room, turned to her grandmother, and sheepishly said, "I'm not sure what to do, but I want to do something. Can you wait here and give me some time?" She nodded slowly with a worried look on her face and continued with her knitting.

I went back to the art room and started cleaning the brushes Brandy had been using to paint. I was trying to come up with an idea. Then a text from Brandy came up on my phone: "I'm at the park."

I started to march out the door to fetch her at the park so we could talk. I could feel myself embody my telltale stance of rigidity, so I stopped myself. I'd felt it many times before while working with Brandy. If I walked straight out to talk with her, I wouldn't be collaborating—I would be confronting. I would forfeit any chance of talking about her reaction to our conversation, and instead I'd give her another opportunity to thrash authority and repeat the pattern that had brought her to therapy in the first place. I had learned from her that if I was going to maintain our relationship, I had to trust her process and allow her to lead a bit. Taking her cue was sometimes a bigger challenge than I liked to face, but I decided to stay flexible.

"How many roosters do you see?" I texted. (My office is located in a small town where wild roosters and chickens roam the park.)

"Lots, and there's one that hopped up on the bench with me. Weird," she texted back.

We texted about the kids she saw swinging and climbing on the jungle gym. She told me about the old people doing Tai Chi on the grassy hill. I told her about cleaning the brushes and putting her painting up to dry.

I went out to the waiting room and told Brandy's grandmother that we were continuing the session via text. She smiled with relief.

Eventually Brandy brought up her reaction. "I get sick to my stomach and want to vomit when I think about the fighting."

"It's hard stuff to talk about," I reflected. "I wish I could see how your face looks right now."

She immediately sent a selfie—index finger stuck halfway down her open mouth, eyes squinted in pain.

I selfied back—hand on heart, head tilted in compassion.

She sent a smiley face.

I told her that it was time for her to meet her grandmother in the parking lot and go home. And she did. Our next several sessions were spent outside with my camera. Brandy's portraits said more than any of her texts or spoken words could say. Once again, our collaboration took us to a place that neither of us could have gone alone, and I added another layer to my understanding of that strip of paper message from Susan Orr. "Try trusting the Art" meant trusting the therapeutic process and staying in malleable collaboration with my client.

There were several more moments like these between me and Brandy. In my work with her, I practiced navigating Flexible Commitment over and over again. When those moments happened, when my plan had lost its way and the outcome I had envisioned was no longer clear, I had to consciously surrender to the process. For the sake of our therapeutic relationship, I had to coax myself out of the wish to force the agenda, and instead relax. I had to revisit my Initial Idea and join Brandy in her brilliant process. When I did, we ended up creating moments that had never been experienced before. I am grateful for the practice and for the unique experiences that Brandy and I had as a result.

The Importance of Flexible Commitment

Once we enter the fourth stage of the creative process, we are well into creating. We are engaged with our art, our client, our process. But, as demonstrated in my sessions with Brandy, the process is inherently unpredictable. Things rarely go as planned, and we have to be ready to change and adjust accordingly. When we are able to stay nimble, we continue to navigate the creative process without getting stuck. Often this allows us blissful moments of Flow (the fifth stage). If we can't stay resilient and move through these changes, the therapeutic process and the creative process come to a screaming halt. Things feel stagnant. We miss out on Flow. And, most importantly, we lose our commitment to the client and are no longer helpful in the therapeutic relationship.

What Flexible Commitment Requires

- Perseverance
- Hanging out in the neutral zone
- Treating mistakes as opportunities.

Perseverance

It's 1:05. No Blake. I text him: "On your way?" No response.

It's 1:10. No Blake. I text him: "I'm missing you today." No response.

It's 1:50. No Blake, no text from him. I call him and leave a voicemail. "I missed you today. What happened? Will I see you on Thursday?"

At 1:53, he texts me. "Sorry, I'm a fuckup. I slept through my alarm. I'll be there Thursday."

I text him, "Looking forward to seeing you Thursday."

Maybe I'd see him, maybe I wouldn't. But on Thursday, if he didn't show, I'd go through the same routine. He never went longer than a week without showing up.

This interaction was typical for Blake at the beginning of therapy. When I first met him ten years ago, he was a pot-smoking high-school dropout who balked at authority. His relationships were insecure attachments fraught with entitlement, blame, and betrayal. Everywhere he turned, he was disappointed by people. His disappointment extended to himself, which resulted in a sizable collection of failed goals and an unwieldy sense of inadequacy. His future didn't look very bright, and he suffered long periods of depression as a result. The psychologist who referred Blake had recommended residential treatment, but he had refused to go and his parents weren't sure that residential was the right choice.

Instead, Blake began coming to see me twice a week for a mix of art therapy and talk therapy. The work we did was incredibly challenging. While there were all kinds of issues, the main one was the complicated attachment template that he brought to our relationship. He would no-show in an erratic pattern that seemed intractable. It stretched my ability to stay in relationship with him. I didn't know if I was doing the right thing by keeping him as a client. There wasn't a week that went by in those first two years that I didn't ask myself whether I should refer him to someone else. I wasn't sure I was helping, and there were times when my doubt got the better of me. Nevertheless, I didn't give up. I stayed committed to our work and didn't throw away the connection I thought I could hold onto in our relationship.

Those early missed appointments were agonizing for me. I would plan a session only to have him no-show. Then I'd have to figure out what my next idea or plan was going to be. How many times could I maintain a sense of Flexible Commitment and stop myself from giving up? But eventually I came to peace with these doubts. Instead of feeling stuck, I decided that I would hold space for Blake even while he wasn't there. If he no-showed, I'd text him and tell him that I missed seeing him, and then, rather than catching up on paperwork or returning a few calls, I'd think about him. I'd imagine him oversleeping or forgetting or just being him. Sometimes I'd paint, sometimes I'd knit.

When he showed up for a session, I would tell him or show him what I did during his absence. I'd show him evidence of the space that he took up even while he was gone. Eventually, his no-shows turned into requests for a phone session. He would text and let me know that he didn't have gas money to come to my office or that his alarm hadn't woken him up, but he still wanted to engage. Eventually we arrived at a wonderful rhythm of him showing up every week, on time, ready to work. This took a long time—a couple of years, actually. It was challenging to ask myself every time he didn't show up whether I was doing the right thing. But the bond that we had formed was foundational to Blake's willingness to look closely at his relationships with others. His trust in our relationship was evident in his willingness to delve honestly into the family dynamics that burdened him. He brought difficult choices to session and we would discuss them at length. Gradually, he was able to slow down his impulsive reactions and use me to process them. In our work, his intelligent and insightful mind began to shine. I'd held space for him, which allowed him to come to session and fill it when he was ready.

I've worked with Blake on and off over the years after his initial treatment. He remains one of my most earnest and hard-working clients. I am grateful to him and the choice that I made to stay committed to our process. As a result, I am better at navigating these potential stuck places with others.

There have been other clients with whom I couldn't ethically sustain this kind of commitment. I've told many a parent that I wouldn't see their child because the child wasn't willing to participate in therapy. And I've certainly been in the role of consulting where I've encouraged a therapist to refer a client. This is a true dilemma for all artists and in all creative endeavors. When should you hang in despite the doubts and frustrations? When should you admit defeat or failure and move on to the next endeavor? It's tough to decide. Therapists everywhere grapple with this edge. We want our work to benefit the client, and yet, sometimes our sessions don't give us clear ideas about whether we are helping. We can ask the client, we can ask consultants, we can ask ourselves; many times there isn't a definitive answer.

I liken this dilemma to the act of writing. It's a universally accepted idea that an author is not going to write something of value every single time she sits down. The day may be hugely productive or a complete waste—it's unpredictable. There may be pages of good content or just a sentence worth preserving. Despite this knowledge, a writer sits down and does the work. She writes what she can, engages in whatever way is possible. And here's the really great thing: the wise writer knows that even the days that she produces complete waste, she's done something of value. She may not have word product, but she might have cleared the way for something good to come. She may have stepped closer to the stuff that is masterful and transformative.

And if we accept that every therapy session is not going to result in a masterpiece or an "aha" or a tangible shift, we need to have some gauge that tells us when to maintain the commitment to hanging in despite it all. There is certainly a time and place when we need to pull the plug and refer, when we have to make a distinction between creative process and just not helping. But it's hard. With Blake, I learned how much of a practice my therapy work really is, and how rewarding it can be if I stick with it. Susan Orr's statement, "Try trusting the Art," helps me tune in and make that choice between sustained practice and realistic defeat.

Hanging Out in the Neutral Zone

Sandy's striking beauty was evident even behind her sunken, dark eyes. She came to see me days after a tragic accident had killed her baby and her husband. She dragged herself to my office, shoulders curved inward in an attempt to bear the burden of her grief. She said the only place she could tolerate was her closet, where, knees to chest, head in hands, she would re-create the memories that marked a time before the tragedy. She said she couldn't stop thinking about her old dreams—the ones that seemed practical and realizable, the ones that she had lived for and strived for. She would wish with all her might to go back in time so she could just pick up where she had left off. She wanted to raise the baby, nurture her connection with her soulmate, thrive in her promising new career. Every time she thought these thoughts, she'd scream with the pain as if it had just happened.

In my work with Sandy, I truly had to improvise. There is no bulletproof formula for recovering from this sort of grief. The outcome is vague. What does "recovered" look like to someone whose life has been so drastically altered? And yet I held hope for a sense of freedom from her burden and an ability to exist without excruciating pain. I didn't know how I would help her get there, and I didn't know the exact outcome of our work together. But, in the most creative way possible, we worked.

Some days her art reached back to the dreams she had begun to taste: the warmth of her new baby and his father in the nest of their extended family; Mama in her glory, radiant with love. Other days she could imagine another baby, as perfect and new as her first had been, this time healthy and strong with more days ahead of him. She would sigh at this representation of a new dream, evidence that she had been through the worst and come out the other side.

But most days, she was in between, on a tightrope where it seemed as impossible to go back to the start as it did to get to the other side. She was in transition, caught between the old and the new. We called those times "stuck in the neutral zone." Working in the "neutral zone" became an essential part of her healing. And yet I wanted to lure her from her neutral zone to the other side, where new possibility could give her a foothold and start her on her way again. I wanted to prescribe homework that would nudge her along so that her closet times would be replaced by hope and joy and new radiance for life. I wanted to dangle a new picture so that she would claim it as her own: take a running start, leap into it, and make it true.

But I didn't. I hung out in the neutral zone. I knew that if I forced the exact outcome with Sandy, I would stop her recovery. So I thought up ways to connect with her in the neutral zone. I improvised. It was impossible to plan sessions because I didn't know how Sandy would be feeling on any given day. I resisted thinking up activities crafted to strategically move her in the right direction. Instead, we'd meet; we'd talk; sometimes we'd make art. Despite the discomfort, I felt a strong obligation not to steer, but instead to find ways to meet her where she was, moment to moment.

One time Sandy brought me a latte and I suggested we have a tea party. We spread a tablecloth on the floor and set two extra places, one for her husband and one for her son. We told them stories in English accents and teared up at the tenderness of the moment we shared. Another time she brought in her son's baby book. I suggested she add to it during our session and she ended up painting an outline of her hand in "sunny" yellow on the last page.

She learned to give her closet times space. They became times of recognizing that she was midway in this transition, and that she didn't have to force herself to solidify her end goal. There were times when she wanted help envisioning a future and collecting options. I made sure she knew she didn't have to decide, conclude, or plan. She could just brainstorm and tolerate the terror of "in between" and improvising. I was awed by her creativity. Her passion for nurturing others shone through all of her options: a pet rescue organization, a community farm, a developmental psychology degree, a marriage retreat center, adopting a dozen kids from Russia, an artist co-op, writing her story to inspire others.

Every time there was a new list of options (with the rule that none were too "out there" to be considered), I recognized the parallel in my own art practice. The first colors I slapped onto that blank canvas had endless possibilities—mind-boggling invitations. The freedom to start was followed by the freedom to explore. I found that when I held that neutral zone as sacred, I could delay the rush to finish, and instead, delight in creative expansion and improvisation. In fact, I started to think about rushing to finish as chickening out. It was much easier to simply choose a direction than to face the fear of not quite knowing, hanging out a bit, and expanding into creative possibility.

Once Sandy allowed her grief the spaciousness it needed rather than rushing to fill in another life picture, she started to engage in the same activity with her art. She would allow herself to express her pain and suffering without having to know where this new drawing or painting would take her. She became good at improvising, too. If she couldn't plan, then at least she could allow things to come in the moment.

Slowly, her art began to reflect this resilience—her newfound ability to just hang out in the unknown. It could be sad but not repellent. It could be forceful but not pushy. As a result, she was able to begin the process of emerging from the "neutral zone" and face that very difficult transition to her new life. Now, in her updates, she has let me know that she has continued to face transitions in a similarly beautiful way. Her respect for transition time has carried forward. She and her new husband share a mutual patience about when to start a family. She holds on to the value of "hanging out in the neutral zone."

As therapists, we often have a hard time joining our clients in this neutral zone. To hang out with them midway across the tightrope is to tolerate not-knowing. To let go of the exact outcome and admit we don't know requires deep trust in the process of change. When we embrace this place as part of our creative process like Sandy did, we learn resilience. When we teach that not-knowing isn't a deficit in experience, but rather a state of learning and change, we remain hopeful. And when change and creativity go hand in hand, transition, even in the neutral zone, becomes an amazingly beautiful part of life.

Treating Mistakes as Opportunities

When we look at the therapeutic process as a creative process, we are invited to look at mistakes as an artist or innovator would. Mistakes do not have to mean failure. Instead, they can be, in James Joyce's words, "portals of discovery." I am not suggesting that we remove the precautionary brake altogether and forget our training, experience, and ethical obligations. Rather, I'm suggesting that we ease up a bit on that brake and embrace the imperfection that comes with recognizing our humanness. In the Introduction, we looked at our profession's error-phobic culture and how it negatively impacts our work as a whole. In the fourth stage of the creative process, we can look at how treating mistakes as opportunity allows us not only to avoid the trap of collapsing into a sense of failure and defeat, but also to change direction when we need to.

In the realm of innovation, many miraculous discoveries are the result of mistakes. John Pemberton invented a medicinal syrup meant to help with exhaustion and headaches, and when his assistant accidently mixed it with carbonated water, Coca-Cola was born. In 1928, scientist Alexander Fleming noticed that mold spores had contaminated one of the bacteria samples he had left by an open window. Instead of throwing it away, he took a close look and noticed the mold was dissolving harmful bacteria; in this way, he discovered penicillin. Constantin Fahlberg failed to wash his hands one night after working in his lab; when he sat down to dinner and tasted an inexplicable sweetness, he realized he had accidentally discovered saccharin (Kreuger, 2010). If these innovators hadn't treated their mistakes as opportunities, they would not have contributed all that they did.

This approach to mistakes nearly invites failure as an essential part of creativity. Picasso said, "With me a picture is a sum of destructions. I make a picture, and proceed to destroy it." With each destruction, Picasso believed his finds became more substantial; in the end, his extraordinary paintings were what he called "the result of rejected discoveries" (Zervos, 1952).

Whether it's mistakenly asking a question of your client, like the one I asked of Brandy that sent her off to the park, or visibly struggling to tolerate the excruciating level of despair that a grieving client like Sandy experiences, we therapists need to put these moments to use. We need to know how to weave them into the fabric of our therapy sessions without blaming our clients or collapsing with our own failure.

Mistakes aren't inherently bad. In fact, psychologist Ellen Langer's research offers an explanation about the relationship between mistakes and enjoyment. When she deliberately caused writers and artists to make mistakes midway through a creative activity and then instructed them to keep going and integrate the mistake, the results were fascinating. Not only did the artists and writers enjoy the activity more than those in the control group who didn't make mistakes, but their finished product was rated much better by judges. Langer (2005: p. 84) observed, "Our aversion to mistakes may be a result of mindless learning of rules."

As therapists, one of the most common "mistakes" is misattunements, or what psychoanalyst Heinz Kohut termed empathic failures. In Kohut's (1984) conception, no therapist, however experienced or skilled, will accurately understand a client's internal world in every moment. Moreover, if we treat an empathic failure as an opportunity to deconstruct and revise our mistake, we can come to an even more powerful place of empathy and understanding. Kohut believed that these kinds of mistake are actually vital to the development of a healthy therapeutic alliance.

Emily, a therapist in a handwork circle that I facilitated, shared a powerful moment of empathic failure with our group. She had been working with Daniel, a young man who was experiencing panicky feelings associated with going away to college. Daniel had been describing his worries during one session. After she thought she had empathized with him, she began trying to shift his negative thinking to envision other possible outcomes of living with a roommate for the first time. He became agitated and loudly complained, "You aren't hearing me. You don't understand."

As she told this story, Emily put her hand up to her heart and told us that he had been exactly right. She hadn't been hearing him, even though she'd thought that she had. In that instant, she stopped her attempts to shift his thinking and said to him, "I skipped over way too much, didn't I? I'm so sorry. I've got to slow down this train I get on because it does you no good." They spent a few moments in silence. Then her client spontaneously raised a bent arm as if he were a train conductor, pumped it in the air, and teased, "Choo-choo!"

Emily laughed. Her client laughed. Our handwork circle laughed. Emily had treated her mistake as an opportunity to apologize and to have her client experience her as human. She had also used the moment of silence as a way of joining him again, without her agenda. The experience deepened their understanding of one another and even provided some shared humor that they could use as a way to move into the next part of the session.

Therapist and author Jeffrey Kottler reminds us that we make mistakes all the time. He says that, in fact, "truly exceptional therapists can actually make more mistakes than others, or at least are more inclined to admit to them" (Kottler and Carlson, 2014: p. 129). It is what we *do* about those mistakes that makes every difference in the world. He suggests that becoming intrigued by mistakes and tackling them with relish is the stance that we need to take.

It is unfortunate that many of us haven't been shown how to be intrigued by our mistakes or how to relish failure. Most of the videos of master therapists at work and training tapes depict successes and leave out the mistakes. We don't get to see live-action acknowledgment of mistakes, and we certainly don't get to hear these therapists forgive themselves for their errors. Yet I know that behind closed doors, we are all grappling with our failures and stuck places. The fourth stage of our creative process invites us to look at our mistakes differently and to treat them as opportunities.

This Girl Wanted to Get Chewed Out!

Tasha Norris Bryant is an extraordinary social worker who inspired me to keep trying new things despite failure after failure. She and I worked together at a homeless teen center and school. I was in charge of facilitating a weekly art therapy group and consulting with the staff. She was the lead worker in charge of just about everything else. When Tasha walked into the center every morning, heads turned. No matter what they had been doing, the teens who already knew her ran to her. The ones who had been doing well shared their successes and she celebrated with them, tousling hair, giving high fives. The ones who had been "screwing up" hung their heads sheepishly while she put her arm around them, encouraging, reassuring. Tasha was captivating in her commitment to these kids. She was beautiful and warm, pushy and mean. She used all of herself to get these teens into better life situations. She was deeply committed, and I never saw her try the identical approach twice.

Monique was a young woman at the shelter who had been adopted as a toddler from Russia. Fifteen years old, she had ended up with us after her mom had given her a one-way bus ticket, sent her to live with relatives, and then disappeared. Monique never found the relatives and lived on the streets for several months before Tasha's outreach worker found her. Her adoptive mother had been found dead from an overdose, so the team provided Monique with food and clothes while she lived at the shelter and went to school. Tasha would meet with Monique and talk about boys and birth control and promiscuity and prostitution. When that didn't seem to go very far, she would change the subject to discuss nail polish or basketball or the care of the ducks at the pond. Tasha took Monique for medical and dental checkups and started a search for Monique's birth certificate and any relative who would respond. Monique stayed distant from all of us, mostly reading her books in a corner.

Monique wouldn't do her schoolwork, so Tasha started a book club that consisted of her and Monique. There was a month where I came in for the weekly art therapy group and found Tasha and Monique in the same positions on the couch reading *Smashed* as if they hadn't budged the entire time I was gone. Monique's hygiene was still terrible, so Tasha made her shower and took her for a manicure, pedicure, and makeover at the mall. Tasha was on a mission; she wasn't going to let this traumatized teen float away. She wanted to get Monique to buy into something better than prostitution as a way of life. But anything she tried seemed to be a dead end. Monique still read in the corner. She still stared into space during class. We were all worried for her. But Tasha didn't give up.

Then one day about three months after Monique had come to the shelter, everything changed. I arrived a little late for group only to find the center empty except for Tasha and Monique. I walked in and could feel the thick vibration of grief and anger. Tasha was talking loudly, her face very close to Monique's. "If you don't change your tune, you are going to end up just like your mom. And that is going to kill me."

Monique stared at Tasha, tears streaming down her face.

"It would kill me to hear you'd been found dead somewhere. I wouldn't know what to do with myself." She jabbed at the air with her pointer finger in front of Monique's face. "You have to snap out of it, girl, and start living. I'm not going to let you off the hook anymore. I've had it. You understand?"

Monique collapsed into Tasha's arms, sobs taking up the whole room. Tasha turned to me while hugging Monique and said, "I guess after all the things we tried and failed at, this girl wanted to get chewed out." I smiled at Tasha's magic. She had a knack for scolding in a loving way. Monique soaked it in like she'd been starved.

Monique came to art group that morning with a grin on her face and bragged, "Tasha went off on me!" It was the first time she actually engaged in the art activity and marked the beginning of many more good choices she would make.

Tasha was excellent at what she did with those teens. She allowed herself to fail more times than she succeeded and never let her failures stop her. Tasha loved her job. Interestingly, her love for her job was likely tied into the way in which she reacted to these failures. It was as if she expected the dead ends and collected them like feathers in her cap. The more feathers she collected, the more determined she became to find another way. Her creativity was clearly at the forefront of her work, and her ability to stay committed yet flexible was an inspiration. She didn't let herself get blocked in the fourth stage of the process because every time she didn't succeed, she'd begin again, take a different direction, and find something new.

How to Get Better at Flexible Commitment

Don't Miss Zebras in Your Backyard

One spring night several years ago, my family and I were all on the couch relaxing. It was the last evening of spring break and we were gearing up to go back to work and school the next day. We were tired and satiated with family time and our trip to the snow that day, and I knew if I didn't get my kids off to bed, the next morning was going to be difficult. As my two youngest, aged 12 and 9, sprawled on the couch, my husband picked my head up off of his shoulder to answer the doorbell. It was about 9 p.m., too late for a visitor in our quiet neighborhood. So it made sense (in a very odd way) that my husband opened the door to a sheriff deputy.

I didn't hear their conversation clearly because I had started to prod the kids into getting up to brush their teeth for bed. My husband returned to the couch and informed us calmly, "There is a zebra in our backyard and the sheriff wants us to keep the dogs inside."

My kids popped up from the couch like two jack-in-the boxes, asking, "Can we see the zebra? Can we see the zebra?"

My husband told us that the zebra was running loose in the easement between our property and the neighbors' and that it was just outside our backyard fence. Sam headed for the back door.

"Wait a minute, buddy," I told him firmly. "You can't go out there. The sheriff told us to stay away, and we have to respect that." Somewhere in the corners of my parental expectations map, I told myself that this was good moral messaging and went on to tuck them both into bed.

As I lay in bed myself, I could hear the sheriff outside my bedroom window on his walkie talkie. "I can't believe I almost missed this. I was going to call in sick tonight! I'm going to call you the Zebra Whisperer from now on!" He was talking to his partner who was on the other side of our fence, calling to the zebra like it was a kitty: "Here, zebra, zebra. Here, girl."

My husband had fallen asleep. I was wide awake.

I was lying there, rigid in my rules about getting enough sleep and respecting authority, and my kids were missing meeting a zebra whisperer. I was denying them the chance to witness a zebra being corralled right from their own backyard and to remember it for a very long time.

I got up and got my kids out of bed, and we quietly crept outside. The sheriff eyed my youngest, Sam, and signaled, index finger to his mouth, "Shhhh." Sam mirrored the sheriff, his own index finger in front of his mouth and nodded. We were backyard stalkers, creeping to the fence to see the zebra.

We spent the next two hours in giddy anticipation, watching and listening. At one point we got footstools. At another I went to fetch my camera. The sheriff needed to borrow a flashlight, so my daughter went and found one. I stood on an upside-down bucket, peering over the fence, chastising myself for being so rule-bound and inflexible that I almost missed this extraordinary event.

It was a school night; it was late; we were told not to be there. But the kids and I got to see that zebra running back and forth in her wildness. We got to marvel at her markings so clear and up close. And we got to go to bed late that night knowing that she was safely captured and back on her way to Oregon after a slight detour into our backyard because her trailer door had come open. That night, I vowed that I would seize more opportunities like this and strive to be more flexible.

It might seem obvious that if you had been there, you would have let go of your agenda and rules and allowed the experience to unfold—you would have just gone to see the zebra. If so, that's probably a good sign. But really, how many times do similar occurrences happen with clients? If I hadn't stayed flexible with Brandy, we would never have climbed out the window or texted in the park. Her way of relating to others might not have changed. Instead, we got to exchange funny selfies and have new experiences that helped us both stay unstuck in our creative process. We seized the opportunity, stretched the rules a bit, and benefited in the end.

If we force the agenda when there is a clear invitation to do something different, we get stuck. If we don't seize opportunities that clients extend to us, we risk missing the chance to see a zebra—right in our own backyard.

Go Beyond Words

When a conversation with a client, friend, or colleague isn't going as expected, it is easy for frustration and negative feelings to come rushing in. We can criticize ourselves for not handling the situation the way we intended. We can withdraw or push the other person away. We often end up forming judgments about the other person as a result of the difficult conversation. These reactions are signs that our thinking has become rigid and we are blocked in our creative process because we are so attached to an exact outcome. I often tell the following story to therapists and clients who feel pressure to guarantee a specific outcome in sessions.

It had been too long since I'd visited my grandparents. I'd settled into my post-college life, and weekend visits that had once felt revitalizing now seemed distracting. But my grandfather's Alzheimer's had begun to take him away, and I decided to go visit them before it was too late. I drove the three hours up the coast on new tires Grampa had bought in return for a promise that I'd visit more often. That was before he had started wandering off in the dark and calling the cops in the middle of the night with paranoid fears about my grandmother.

When I arrived, the house flooded me with the wooded smell of fire and moss, so unchanged for decades. My grandparents both wrapped me in their arms, delighted at my arrival. I could do no wrong in their eyes.

Grampa went out to do his daily watering, and I had tea with my beloved grandmother. She told me about her work with the local musicians, how she continued teaching piano despite the increased attention Grampa required. She clapped her huge hands together, holding mine in between, as she heard about my new job, new house, new life. She was proud and told me so.

That evening, I wanted to give the same report to my grandfather. I wanted to tell him all the stories I had catalogued about the butterflies at Natural Bridges State Beach and my cat that had become psychotic after neighbors accidentally locked him in the garage. I wanted to share the joy and accomplishment of having finally made it to a stage in my life where I felt independent and self-sufficient. I imagined he'd be proudest because he had always believed in me.

I didn't get to say any of that. Grampa came upstairs after a nap, squeezed me in a huge bear hug, and started to try to tell me his own story. "My job," he began, and stopped. He tried to write a word in his hand, then said, "It's a long thing . . ." His words weren't there, but his frustration was. He hit a fist into his palm. I held out my hands, hoping he'd stop hitting and soften with my touch. I covered his big hands with mine, feeling the physical strength that hadn't left him like his words had. His blue eyes were framed by the furrowed shelf of eyebrows I'd threatened to trim several years ago. He looked straight through to my heart. I gazed back, not knowing what to say or do. He took hold of my hand and led me outside onto the deck.

The night was cool. The quiet rhythm of the waves soothed us. We watched the bats fly out from the eaves, into the treetops and out over the ridge. The scent of the bay trees wafted up to our perch. Then Grampa pointed with the hand not holding mine. A luminous moon began to appear from behind the distant hills. We watched silently as it climbed to streak the water and light a pathway that connected miles of bay and mountain and sand. I looked up at him and saw that he'd been looking at me—no more frustration in the furrow of his brow, just love and joy in a moment shared.

When we'd first walked out to the deck, I had thought maybe I would just carry on, even if he wouldn't listen, and tell him all

I had brought to share. I was about to, but then I relaxed and recognized that there was a different way. His way now was not through words. It was beyond words, with the moon and the water, and holding hands with someone he loved. The moon we saw that night was more beautiful than any I had ever seen before or since. And I am forever grateful for my Grampa's Flexible Commitment. Even when words failed him, he found a way to stay in conversation with me.

This was a powerful experience for me and especially hard because of how important my grandfather had been to me. But even when this misstep or block occurs in sessions with clients, it can feel as if solid ground has betrayed us. We can feel like we've lost our way and have nothing to fall back on. When this happens, I like to remember Grampa's full moon and relax in knowing that the art of relationship doesn't have to follow any specific template. If we've lost our way, as long as we stay flexible and committed, we can find it again in unexpected places.

Flexible Commitment with Clients

A Creative Pesponse to Anger

Jen was a 15-year-old schizoaffective client who liked to play dress-up. She and I had had a rough start due to the fact that I didn't have oil paints in my studio. She announced that "real artists use oil paint," and concluded that because I didn't have any oils, this meant I was not a real artist and probably couldn't help her. She kept coming, albeit reluctantly. Some days she was dressed as a ballerina; others she was a firefighter. Each day I saw her, she had fresh cuts on her arms and dark circles under her eyes. We worked together twice a week for several months. She fell in love with the painting wall where she could pin a large piece of paper and splatter paint as much as she wanted. She loved the Prang Tempera I supplied for these colorful expressions. She took to calling it "Pro Pigmented Paint"—always making the quotation marks with her fingers in a sarcastic gesture—because of how it was described on the container's label.

A couple of months into treatment, her cutting incidences had decreased. Her interest in her future increased. Her meds were finally sorted out. She was doing a bit better and I was less worried than I had been when we first met. One day during this period, Jen came to session dressed like she was going to a rodeo, complete with kerchief and metal spurs. She flopped on the couch and said, "Death to the Pro Pigmented Paint." This time she didn't include the quote gesture with her fingers. She was dead serious.

I smiled and even giggled a tiny giggle. "What?"

That was all she needed to absolutely let loose. "You are not a real artist," she yelled. "You do not have oil paints. I can't believe you have this whole façade set up and no one else sees through it. You conned me into it and I'm not going to do it anymore." I made a mental check to see whether my colleague had told me she was coming into the office today to see clients. It would be entirely too loud for her.

Before I could say anything, Jen continued, "You are paid to care, so this whole thing is fake. You just take my parents' money and think nothing of it all. I can't stand it. I can't stand you. I will not use Pro Pigmented Paint and I don't think you can help me anymore." She hit the sofa with both of her hands for emphasis.

I couldn't find anything to say that sounded good. I didn't want to attack her back. I didn't want to try to convince her to think differently about me and about therapy. I didn't want to manipulate. I thought desperately, *What would a real therapist do in this situation?*

And then I felt a softening. My heart had been beating fast and as I relaxed, it slowed. My chest flushed and my hands warmed. I looked into Jen's eyes. They were sparkling and alive. A thought popped into my mind: *Don't force things. Embrace it, don't stop it.*

I took a breath and matched her intensity, "Can you feel it? Can you feel the incredible energy that you've brought here?

Man, it's unbelievable. Sure you're angry, but you're also passionate and alive!"

She stuck out her tongue at me and squished up her face.

I made a similar face back to her, placing my hands on my cheeks in order to frame it.

She returned another, this time pulling her mouth wide with her fingers.

I pushed up my nose and opened my mouth as wide as it would go.

We continued back and forth for a while without saying a word. Once she laughed a sweet laugh when my fishy face made sucking noises.

The tingling diminished. The energy started to calm. She looked more settled.

It was time for her to go. "See you on Thursday?" I said.

"Of course, silly. Get the Pro Pigmented Paints ready." And she left, her fingers still gesturing the sarcastic air quotes they always had.

That session could have gone any number of ways. I might have kicked her out for being so rude. I might have told her that she was right—that if she felt that way about me, I couldn't help her. I might have tried to change her mind and ask her for another chance. I could have pointed out to her that this was the same dysregulated state that got her into trouble and led to cutting at home. I could have attempted to coach her to ground herself with breathing or other forms of mindfulness. All of these would have been decent responses, grounded in various therapeutic constructs.

But staying true to my creative process, I pulled an idea from the here-and-now—one that brought me to brand new territory, one that included Jen in a collaborative way and didn't make me feel rule bound or rigid. I made myself flexible—literally, with my faces, and figuratively, in my responses. Jen responded in kind—always creative and different.

Later, when we laughed about that day, Jen told me that I had surprised the heck out of her. She had expected me to kick her out and thought that she deserved it. It was what she wanted. But, in the end, she was happy that I had responded in such an unexpected way. She had never experienced her anger as alive and passionate. She told me that I had taught her something entirely new and that she wanted to continue to find out more. Our ability to navigate this potential stuck place that day served us well. We were able to do it in many other instances, which increased her resilience in the face of difficult emotions and validated the importance of my staying both flexible and committed to the process.

Summary

Flexible Commitment is a challenging stage of the creative process. It requires that we remain fully engaged even in the face of mistakes. It asks us to be nimble in our approach and to be open to new ideas. Sometimes this stage invites us to try things we've never tried before and we need to embrace this in service of the process. To navigate Flexible Commitment means we are able to trust the process and, in so doing, inevitably reap the reward of the next stage, Flow.

Questions to Ponder

1. What does it feel like when you force things in therapy? What does it sound like, look like, taste like?
2. What does it feel like when you surrender in therapy? What does it sound like, look like, taste like?
3. Think of a time when you had to improvise rather than follow the plan. How did it go?
4. Think of a client with whom you've recently felt stuck. How might being flexible and not knowing the exact outcome of your sessions play a part in getting unstuck?

Art Invitations

The following art activities are designed to assist you in practicing Flexible Commitment. When you can navigate mistakes, change direction, and simultaneously stay engaged with these art activities, you can use the same muscle to navigate your therapeutic process.

Happy Accidents

In this art activity, you are invited to be freed from having to copy exactly what you see and, instead, watch for gestures and marks that are uniquely yours. When you are attuned to the happy accidents, you are more likely to be relaxed and using nimble thinking. This will serve you in session when things aren't going as planned and you need to prevent yourself from getting blocked in Flexible Commitment.

Here's what you need:

- Drawing paper
- Painting or drawing implements: pencil, marker, etc.

Here's how:

1. On your paper, begin to draw a grid. Don't plan it out, just watch it take shape in whatever way it happens.
2. Once you have a grid on your page, look at it and notice any imperfections, inconsistencies, or what I would call "happy accidents." For instance, the lines may not be straight or the squares may not be equal. Play with these inconsistencies by augmenting them or embellishing them. See if you can feel a sense of lightness, flexibility, even humor in your play.
3. What was it like to bring play into your grid? Could you let go and have fun with the "happy accidents"?

Figure 6.1 Shelley's "Happy Accident"

Shelley's grid was not really what she had in her mind's eye. She said, "This grid isn't exactly plotted out. I ran out of space to make the same sized squares. This could be a happy accident in the sense that I really don't want to control all of the elements." She thought of times when she's anticipated something in therapy, but then there has been a "blip that is different than what I anticipated." She recognizes those "blips" as potentially pivotal moments. "They can lead to something really important and I don't want to cover them up or start over." Instead, Shelley tends to ask herself, "What do I do with this?" In that sense, she loved that her grid reminded her to stay resilient even in her mistakes.

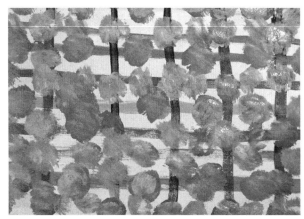

Figure 6.2 Susan's "Happy Accident" (see color version in plate section)

When Susan was painting her grid she noticed a tiny drip. She decided to make the drip her "happy accident." She kept going and added blobs and circular swirls with her brush. The new layers and colors were invitations for her to play with her painting. She reflected on her experience: "I want to make more of those moments in my art and my work. For me, they are about letting the new content come in with curiosity, openness, and interest. As long as I stay light and playful, these moments can be breaths of fresh air."

Mosaics

This activity gives you the opportunity to practice construction, deconstruction, and reconstruction, which are part of the process of changing direction and detaching from the exact outcome. It also invites you to take a look at your natural problem-solving methods, which can be utilized when you find yourself stuck in session.

Here's what you need:

- Paper
- Drawing materials
- Glue.

Here's how:

1. Think of a client with whom you feel stuck. Draw a representation of this stuck feeling. It can just be the stuck feeling in abstract, or it can be a depiction of the struggle that's keeping you stuck. It doesn't have to look like something identifiable as long as it conveys your sense of being stuck.
2. Now write down some words that go with your picture.
3. Take your picture and tear it into pieces. This is the deconstruction part.
4. Get a new piece of paper and, using the pieces of paper that you tore, piece together a new picture. You might have to play with the arrangement for a while before it gels into a new image. Pay attention to your choices at this point. What does your internal narration or dialogue sound like? Glue the pieces down in their new arrangement.
5. If you need to add more color at this point to fill in the spaces, do so.
6. Write down some words that go with your new picture.
7. Compare you old with your new. Think or journal about the following questions: How did you figure out what to do with the pieces? What questions did you ask yourself? What strategy did you use to be able to reconstruct your picture? The

answers to these questions will reveal how you tend to solve problems. The answers can also be strategies that you remind yourself of in the future when you feel stuck. When you use your strategy, you will be successfully navigating the fourth stage of your creative process.

Figure 6.3 Carly's "Stuck"

Figure 6.4 Carly's "New Perspective"

Carly's art activity happened very easily. When she drew her "Stuck," it was all fitted tightly together. Then she tore the pieces and reassembled them. "When the pieces moved around and started to shift, I had a 'maybe' where the problem might actually start to be solved. I became curious and hopeful." Her willingness to shift perspective and just start from there was a helpful experience. She said, "I want to feel for the shifting lines whenever I encounter a stuck place. This will help me stay flexible with clients."

Figure 6.5 Jamie's "Stuck" (see color version in plate section)

Figure 6.6 Jamie's "New Perspective" (see color version in plate section)

Jamie asked herself, "What else could this be?" as a way of moving from her first drawing to the second. "When I started the second drawing, I realized I didn't have to put it back together exactly the way it was. Then I realized the pieces could go anywhere. Initially the ladder represented no support and this big problem. All of a sudden, the ladder could go anywhere and it became a bridge." Instead of constriction and limited options, Jamie was able to experience energy and excitement. She felt that the question that she used to get this shift, "What else could this be?" helped her turn an obstacle into an opportunity. She expressed enthusiasm for this activity and felt inspired to continue asking herself, "What else could this be?" in her work with clients.

Sustained Painting

This activity invites you to practice the discipline of staying committed to a piece of art while being flexible to what it asks you to change. Because this art activity occurs over a period of time, it invites you to experience the thread that holds the creative process together. Over time, it takes different turns and changes into versions of a painting that you might never have predicted. This is similar to the way treatment can unfold with a client. Allowing the process to change over time is a sustained commitment.

Here's what you need:

- Paper (smallish—5″ x 7″)
- Acrylic paint
- Brushes.

Here's how:

1. Set a timer for 15 minutes and apply paint to your paper. There doesn't need to be any particular intention or topic, just a start. If you feel completely lost for an idea, just make circles with your arm and watch the paint turn into circles. Try to cover the paper without leaving many white spots.
2. Photograph your paper.
3. Repeat this same activity four or five more times. Every time you complete 15 minutes, photograph your painting. You will be painting over the top of your prior painting each time. In some versions, you will still see parts of the old painting; in others, you won't. The idea is not to make the first painting better by adding complementary details. It is to allow a new painting to come from the old painting every time.
4. You may want to write down some of your experiences and how you feel about your painting as you go along. How easy or difficult is it to sustain the commitment to do the activity? Can you stay flexible?
5. Lay out the photos you took alongside your final painting. Reflect on the process. What did you learn? Can you see a thread that runs through all of your paintings? Can you see a relationship or a deepening on a theme?

Figure 6.7a Susan's Sustained
Painting Stage 1

Figure 6.7b Susan's Sustained
Painting Stage 2

Figure 6.7c Susan's Sustained
Painting Stage 3

Figure 6.7d Susan's Sustained
Painting Stage 4 (see color
version in plate section)

Susan's journaling recounts her sustained painting process. "My figures
started to change in the paintings. The process was actually very uncomfortable at points. I could feel myself coming up against, 'Not this again.'
Instead of tensing up or quitting, I stuck with it. For me, play and lightness
are so important to being able to get there. It's like this in doing therapy.
When things aren't quite what I thought they were and there's that point
when I feel like I just don't 'get it' I try not to be so serious about everything and stay in despite the discomfort. And then, when you come out the
other side, when you do 'get it,' it's so important and meaningful."

Figure 6.8a Shelley's Sustained Painting Stage 1

Figure 6.8b Shelley's Sustained Painting Stage 2

(c)

Figure 6.8c Shelley's Sustained Painting Stage 3

(d)

Figure 6.8d Shelley's Sustained Painting Stage 4 (see color version in plate section)

Shelley's journaling captured her experience of staying in the moment without planning ahead. "This activity invited me to just go with the flow of things. It was peaceful. The opportunity to let myself go to that place where I'm not thinking of the next step and am right in the moment felt really good. It was also a process of letting go because my Initial Idea wasn't what it turned out to be. I kept telling myself, 'Stay right here.' In therapy, I think there is a process of getting out of my own way. It's that stepping back and allowing for what is, being present with it, and consciously giving up the agenda. That's where so much of the magic of my work happens."

7

FLOW

While Flow is the fifth stage of the creative process and has distinct attributes separate from the other stages, we can also experience it within any of the other stages. Whenever it is experienced, whether as a substantive block of time or a brief few minutes, Flow marks a moment when we've slipped out of our analytic mindset, sidestepped our theoretical framework, and feel as if something is going very right. Mihaly Csikszentmihalyi, author of the seminal work that defined Flow in popular culture, describes it as an "almost automatic, effortless, yet highly focused state of consciousness" (Csikszentmihalyi, 1996: p. 110).

It is important to understand that Flow is not the goal or finish line of the creative process. Similarly, it is not the goal of a therapy session. We can create art, make important discoveries, and help a client without experiencing Flow. It would be a mistake to correlate creative success with the experience of Flow. It is more helpful to consider Flow an experience that acts as a positive reinforcement for undertaking creative endeavors. Flow spurs us on and rewards us along the way for our courageous undertakings. It is the delicious dessert that tops off an engrossing dining experience.

Most therapists I have talked to light up when they recall moments of Flow with their clients. These are the kinds of moments that we dreamed about having with clients when we started out. Natalie Goldberg (2014: p. 23) describes her sense of Flow this way: "My mind was no longer up in the area above my eyebrows; my mind was my whole body. My hands moved the brush by their own natural force. I worked by instinct, heard cues from the objects in the picture and from my heart and blood vessels." Therapists, too, describe a physical experience of Flow with their clients. The neurological changes often include quickened heartbeat, higher blood pressure, and an intensity of awareness. In Flow, we catch glimpses of our own and our clients' most actualized selves.

For me, this is why Flow is the fifth stage. The creative process asks us to grapple with doubt and fear, to take risks and align with uncertainty, to not know where we are going and trust that something will come of it. And in the end, sometimes, if we are lucky, we are rewarded with the utmost affirmation of life itself – Flow.

If we practice navigating the other four stages of the creative process, and can avoid getting too blocked in those stages, Flow will happen. It is a happy byproduct. It is an occasional reward for the hard work we and our clients have done.

How to Recognize Flow

In order to reap the rewards of experiencing Flow, we need to learn to recognize how it feels when it does happen. We can then celebrate the moment and the fact that we've successfully avoided getting stuck or blocked in our creative process. In Flow, our sense of time becomes suspended. These are the sessions when we look up at the clock and feel amazed that the hour has gone by without our noticing. This sensed loss of time is due to the fact that we enter a state of intense absorption.

We are so intent on the interaction or creative endeavor that awareness and action are merged. Our thoughts, words, and behaviors are so finely attuned that we don't deliberate or even analyze. We have a sense of being in sync with our work and our client. We are alert, yet relaxed. We embody a sense of effortless joy and keen satisfaction.

The following stories and vignettes describe moments of Flow in an effort to shed light on the experience. When we can recognize Flow, we feed our creative work so that it can remain full of vitality.

The Red Fox

The summer before I entered high school, my brother and I made the three-thousand-mile trip to California from our home in Sewickley, Pennsylvania. We were there to visit to our father, and he had dropped us off at our grandparents' house for a couple of weeks. It wasn't so bad, really. There was the Tomales Bay and music recitals and a feeling of being loved and attended to. My obsessive worries about bad skin and boys had been replaced with older people's activities such as listening to opera and polishing silver. And, most importantly, I had agreed to join Grampa on his summer project: we were going to make friends with a red fox.

Grampa's den looked out onto a deck that had steps leading into the woods. The kitchenette and mini-bar of his man cave were fully stocked; we wanted for nothing when we hung out with him in the space where my grandmother refused to go. One entire wall of the cozy room was covered with shelves of opera LPs. Another wall was graced by a larger-than-life Native American sand painting facing the wall of windows that let us peer straight into the woods. His room boasted the only TV in the house, but we didn't watch it that summer. Instead, we sat and stared at his orange shag carpet, trying not to move or fall asleep, and summoned patience and hope to help us sustain our nightly friend-making sessions.

Grampa had made a good start on his project before we arrived. He'd spied a red fox on his daily gardening patrol and put a bowl of food for her on the deck. At first she would only eat in the middle of the night, but he'd leave the light on and she got used to seeing him enough so that she would arrive around bedtime. He had decided to save the next steps for us so that we could participate and see her wild beauty for ourselves.

If anyone had asked me whether I wanted to spend my summer vacation sitting still for hours every night waiting for a red fox to arrive, I would have said, "No way." I had activities that I loved, like knitting and reading and drawing, that I didn't have enough time to do during the year. Summer, for me, was the gift of flitting from one passion to another and filling myself up with creativity. But I loved Grampa dearly, and besides, I wanted to see what would happen.

After dinner each evening, we went down to his den. He put meat in the bowl and placed it on the floor in that night's location. At first, it was right outside the open sliding glass doors. Each night the bowl moved a little farther inside the room, toward his reclining chair. We got settled under our blankets, my brother and I on the couch, Grampa in his chair, and we waited. I counted the strands of orange shag. I tried to breathe slower than my brother. I replayed the entire day start to finish and then backwards. I made up rhymes and rhythms and songs in my head.

And, pretty soon, each evening, the red fox showed up. My thoughts ceased. I felt the snap of my attention come back to the present moment, to the reality that this beautiful creature had arrived. She looked around warily, sniffed towards us, removed a piece of meat from her bowl, and ran away. Another five minutes of nothing, and she'd return. Another glimpse of her. Another moment of intense concentration on her fluffy fur and sharp nose, and she'd be gone again. We did this faithfully for two weeks. I got tired of it, but I loved it all the same.

One evening, Grampa had to go pick up another cousin in San Francisco and left me and my brother in charge of the fox project. She had been arriving consistently every night and eating from her bowl right at Grampa's feet. My brother wanted a night off of "meditative torture," so he went to bed. I filled the bowl and sat in Grampa's chair. It was another long wait. This time I fought the nagging temptation to quit and go read in my cozy bed. I found shapes in the grain of the wood paneling. I tried to move each toe independently. I counted my breaths. Finally, she arrived. She wasn't alone.

Our red fox came up the deck stairs followed by three baby red foxes. My snap to attention was electric. I was afraid that the thumping of my heart would scare her away. She crossed the threshold into the den and made her three little ones wait outside. She looked around, sniffed warily, and then looked me straight in the eye. I flushed with warmth. I wanted to signal my brother to come quick. I wanted Grampa to see. Instead, I sat absolutely still, beaming an internal smile, welcoming the red fox and her babies. She took a piece of meat out to her brood and left it at their feet. They chewed noisily as she returned for her own chunk. She ate at my feet. And I melted into her beauty, taken with this moment.

There were more nights just like this one. Grampa and my brother did get to see the fox babies, and the mama fox even started eating from Grampa's hand. Those moments were beautiful indeed, but not as fully felt as my first night alone with the mama red fox and her babies.

This is such a visceral memory of Flow for me. That summer, I experienced the effortlessness that arrives when we've forgotten ourselves and become a part of a bigger awareness. I was too involved with the fox and the meditative state prior to her arrival to be concerned with failure or disappointment. My intense concentration snapped into place by that mama fox and her babies was indestructible. The fox and I, in my Grampa's den, could have been anywhere in the world, bound by our union, unaware of our surroundings.

These are the moments, in life and in therapy, that keep us going. They are the rewards for long arduous paths taken in conversation, relationships, and projects. They are also evidence that we have navigated the creative process in a beautiful way. We can't force or wish them to happen. While our Flow moments are not always synchronized with our clients' experiences of Flow, whatever way they show up, these moments flood us with a sense of oneness and bliss that feeds us for many more days of effort.

Sing the Body Electric

Flow can happen when we are working alone, but often the experience of Flow is more easily accessed in a group. The collective absorption by group members can feel powerful and intense. Group members will often describe their experience of this shared Flow as tingling and electric. It is as if the group sinks into a shared field of energy when they've arrived at this stage of the creative process.

The first time I remember feeling my body go electric was during band camp my senior year of high school. We were an orchestra of 80 from all around the country, led by an esteemed guest conductor. As we played the open chords of Aaron Copeland's *Appalachian Spring* with full sound, the woodwinds' higher notes flew around our heads, the brass vibrations moved at my feet, and the timpani beat with my heart. I tingled. We flowed.

By myself, playing music was a joy. I did it regularly out of desire and love rather than being forced to practice. I felt my flute could speak for me. But I really didn't feel Flow when I practiced alone. My high school band wasn't terrible, but we were far from Flow. It wasn't until band camp that I came to know how it felt to be pulled in by others to something bigger than myself. When everyone was working in sync to form a cohesive sound, my whole nervous system was on fire. That summer, I learned that Flow was something powerful. I learned to give myself over to it and surrender.

I have a keen sense of that feeling today. In groups and trainings I lead, there is invariably a precious moment when a group drops in. I can't see it coming, but when it arrives, there's a feeling of sinking in, a sense of gelling. The cohesion and synthesis of common energy is tangible. It is reviving and inspiring. When I point it out to participants, they look up at me and smile because they recognize it, too.

A Second Wind

Kate was referred to me by her primary therapist because they both felt she could benefit from expressing and regulating her emotions nonverbally. She was a middle-aged woman who had squelched herself into a powerless nurturer. For the majority of her life, Kate had eschewed anger and confrontation for caretaking and love. She was delightful, sweet, and compassionate. But when she was wronged or hurt, she deflated into an agonized fallen angel. Her early experiences of being criticized had taught to her to shut down rather than add to the aggressiveness of which she had been a victim. She never wanted to hurt others like she'd been hurt. By the time she came to work with me, she had almost erased herself trying to please everyone.

Part of our work together involved finding ways Kate could express anger without experiencing the accompanying guilt and self-deprecating thoughts. I had been helping Kate express emotions in her art for many months. She was able to make drawings and paintings that depicted parts of herself that she had thrown away or left unacknowledged for years. She was a sailboat floating freely in the ocean; she was a goddess emanating light that shined like stained-glass windows in an Italian cathedral; she was a vast, awe-inspiring canyon that stretched on through time. She had been starting to get a foothold out of her depression, and I had had ideas of starting to talk about decreasing the frequency of our sessions and heading toward termination.

But there was a nagging feeling inside me that I had to pursue. I couldn't help imagining what her anger looked like. She was afraid of it taking over, and I had provided safe containment throughout our sessions to make sure this didn't happen.

I had sensed her strength in the hugs with which she greeted me at the start of each session, but I had never really seen her express it on paper. I had the sense that in striving to control her anger, she had stifled her own power. I wanted her to give herself permission to express her anger in order to extricate her self-confidence. In keeping with my own creative process, I felt it was necessary to present her with my idea and have her decide whether she would like to pursue it, too.

So during one session, I suggested she express her anger in paint. Kate was wary of this idea. She thought she might get stuck or regress. But she also sensed how volatile her anger was, and she wanted to stop having to feel so vigilant when she did get angry. So she agreed.

I wanted to give Kate the opportunity to use her whole body, so I got out the biggest brushes I have in the studio. They are large round brushes that are nearly indestructible. I invited Kate to tack a 24-by-36-inch piece of paper on the painting wall. We stood side by side looking at the big white space in front of us.

"This is going to be hard," said Kate, tears already starting down her cheeks.

I felt the two of us perched on an edge of something together. This was a moment of Diving In, and I knew I had to push her, but I also knew the risk was too great for her to bear by herself. So I got directly behind her, nearly touching, and said, "I've got your back."

She hesitated once more. "What color shall I start with?"

"What looks good to you right now?" I replied gently.

She picked up a brush, fisted it into the red paint pot, and used her whole arm to begin to cover the paper. In that moment, her arm might as well have been my arm. I was so intently concentrated on her painting that I was not conscious of my own body.

She started to hit the page with the brush. "Yep," I said as if she were talking to me with her brush. "Slap," went her brush. "Uh huh," I responded. Over and over, until she slowed. We backed away from the page simultaneously. We were doing this one painting together in wordless union.

"Is there more?" I asked.

She picked up a new brush and dipped it in the black. It was runnier than the red, so she splattered it onto the page. Some of the paint flew back onto us. She didn't notice the splotch on my forehead. The black paint landed onto the page and then dripped. As it dripped, she cried. As she cried, I said, "I'm right here with you."

"I feel you," she sobbed. I was so close to her that I felt the air vibrate as her body shook. I took a few breaths to see if I was still grounded and found that I was elated, riveted, and perfectly okay. She hadn't collapsed and neither had I.

"Is there more?" I asked.

"I am so angry," she replied.

"I know. I can see it and feel it. You are so alive right now. This is what you've wanted to let out for a long time."

She went for the dark blue paint and painted fast vertical stripes over half of the page. Her painting was half-jailed in columns of blue. I was still behind her and felt her breathing go steady. Then she said, "No, I don't want to do that anymore!" And she got her red going again—across the page, around the page—full arm movements.

"You're doing great," I told her. "I'm right here. I've got your back." This time I was choked up because she'd reclaimed herself, and I felt the surge of energy that came with it.

I backed up a bit to admire her and her work. She came with me to do the same. We were silently gazing at the rawness in front of us. She was no longer shaking. She went back to the painting and I stayed in my place. This part she was going to do without me. She took a clean brush and dipped it into bright yellow. She placed a large yellow band on the bottom edge of the page. She filled in all of the white space with yellow. She even looked radiantly yellow. She was more beautiful than I'd ever seen her. She stopped and turned to look at me. "One more color and I think it's done."

She took the red brush and I suddenly feared that I hadn't been in sync with her—that I'd been fooling myself into thinking she was okay with all of this intensity. She added a band of red at the very bottom of the page underneath the yellow she had just added.

As she put the brush down, I noticed the yellow splotch of paint on her nose. "Ha!" she said. "Red is both my anger all over the place *and* my foundation. It represents anger and love. It is strength and power and aliveness, just like the yellow." She hugged me with one of her solid hugs. I hugged back, giddy from the intensity of the session and her insight.

"I could never have done that without you," she said. "You truly had my back."

I smiled and sighed as I came back to myself, an art therapist in my studio. I suddenly seemed so ordinary compared to the moment that had just transpired. I felt as if I'd been on a trip to an exotic place where the forces of healing are far stronger than any I could muster on my own. I was a little self-conscious back in the room, and grateful that it was time to wrap up the session.

I asked Kate to take a picture of her painting so that she could remember what she'd made and how the session had transpired. I took a picture too, so that I could do the same.

This session was important for Kate's progress in therapy. It provided her with the felt experience of her own strength and power. It showed her that repressing her anger had shut off the channel to this power, and that, when she opened the channel, it didn't have to be destructive or all consuming. It also came as a result of my following my curiosity. I had followed the sense that there was more we could do, and I invited her into this idea. I had the thought that Kate and I could break through to something bigger together. I invited her to Dive In, despite the fear, and helped her to stay engaged and committed to her process. As a result, we had a powerful shared moment of Flow— one that both of us hold as significant and memorable.

This is often how it feels when we are inching up to an experience of Flow in our creative process: there's a sense if we just went a little further or pushed ourselves a little more, we could enter a different world where time falls away and the trappings of our life no longer weigh us down. My curiosity kept me going with Kate. It asked me to pursue something to which I didn't have an answer. And there was that sense that a second wind was about to come.

Marathon runners describe finding their second wind only after they have exhausted themselves and feel too tired to continue. When their second wind comes, they are able to continue with less strenuous breathing and exertion and they gain the confidence that their body will carry them to the end of the race. This feeling of being set free happens in the creative process, too. Entrepreneur, designer, and teacher David Kelley describes it eloquently: "Opening up the Flow of creativity is like discovering that you've been driving a car with the emergency brake on—and suddenly experiencing what it feels like when you release the brake and can drive freely" (Kelley and Kelley, 2013: p. 4).

After years of partnering with my creative process in a conscious way, I have learned to sense the coming of Flow. If there's curiosity present, it tells me to inch closer and maintain engagement. There is a sense of utter fascination and keen awareness. Distractions disappear. When I begin to feel this happening, like I did after I invited Kate to paint her anger, I've learned to take my foot off the brake and surrender. This is not a free Dive In to selflessness, but a surrender to the wisdom of intuition—the sum of knowledge, experience, and the unconscious. In Flow, the second wind whooshes in and carries us to a place of shared experience that is inaccessible through cognitive or analytical means.

Love, Not Fear

Flow in session does not require the use of expressive arts to happen. It can happen when therapist and client are having a conversation in which they are finely attuned to one another. When the therapist sheds her analytical skin and allows the client's experience to penetrate beyond words, a moment of Flow can be sparked.

Jill was a member of my therapists' handwork circle where we and seven other therapists gathered on a bimonthly basis to knit and embroider while we consulted about cases. Jill had brought up concerns about a client with whom she'd started working in a second round of therapy. Initially she had been seeing Danielle for significant anxiety issues associated with school performance. Danielle had made great progress and was able to enjoy her last year of graduate school, to the point of calling it "the best year of my life." Danielle's life had continued to go well and she began to work full time at a great job in her field. She had returned to therapy with Jill a year later because of an increase in anxiety, specifically related to being away from her adult son.

"I'm frustrated because it feels like all of the good work we did has disappeared," Jill told us. "My client isn't going out now for fear of missing time with her son. It's like her fears are a moving target and I can't get a handle on them."

Jill acknowledged that it was because of her work a year ago with Danielle that her client had been able to enjoy her last year of graduate school and, as a result of this experience, had a greater sense of hope for her future—regardless of the current situation. However, Jill was discouraged. The other therapists in the group who were experienced with seeing therapy as a creative process encouraged Jill to view her work with Danielle through this lens. I reminded Jill that doubt and frustration are normal parts of the creative process. We talked about ways in which Jill could consider this next part of therapy with Danielle as an opportunity to continue working on the same piece of "art" as opposed to trying to start all over again on a new "piece." Jill's trust in her own process helped her go back to her next session with Danielle with enthusiasm for making another connection related to helping Danielle manage her separation anxiety.

When Jill came to our next group meeting, she was giddy. We always start group by sharing and celebrating special moments with clients. Jill was excited to share hers. Jill told us that she had been thinking about Danielle, trying to Incubate, and she found herself curious about a book that Danielle had mentioned. She remembered it had something to do with a character losing her parents, but she wasn't sure. So she took that curiosity into session and asked Danielle.

In response, Danielle retold the story to Jill. It was about a girl whose mom and dad divorced when she was young. In the book, the girl, who was being raised by her mom, went on a search to find her dad because she had lost contact with him. When she did find him, he was dying of cancer and she only had a few days with him. She spent every minute trying to learn about his life and make up for the time that they had lost together.

Jill could see how much this touched Danielle, who had been crying as she retold the story in session. But it didn't make sense to Jill because Danielle had described a very supportive relationship with both of her parents and her son. They were all healthy, active, and a big part of Danielle's life.

Jill asked Danielle more about the book and how it related to her life. Danielle talked about how much the character obviously cared about her parents. She told Jill that the character wanted every minute with her dad, and this had triggered Danielle's fear of losing her son. He was everything to her and she couldn't imagine living without him. She had admitted her worst fear: that something would happen to him and she would have seen him for the last time.

As Jill told us this story, she got a twinkle in her eye. She said with awe in her voice, "At that moment, I felt like I slipped into another zone. I became totally unaware of anything besides myself and Danielle. I could feel Danielle's intense love for her son. I was looking into her eyes and I didn't even question what I was about to say. It just came out. I told her that she was describing *love*, not *fear*."

Jill's twinkle turned to a smile. "I was in that Flow moment, when things seem so right and effortless. I knew I was on to something."

Danielle responded emotionally to Jill's words. Crying, she declared her love for her son and named her love as intense and special, and the most important part of her life. Jill told her again that she was talking about *love*, not *fear*, and that the intensity might feel scary but it was beautiful to see. Jill and Danielle sat quietly nodding at the recognition of the intensity of emotion that they were sharing. It was a Flow moment for sure.

"I feel like I didn't know where I was going with it, but it was important," Jill told us. "It was happening and Danielle and I had to just ride it. There was no therapeutic plan. I just said what I felt and stayed engaged. I love when that happens! It's such a high."

We nodded collectively, as we had all had similar moments with clients.

"Then another thought came to me," Jill told us. "I told Danielle that she was experiencing love even when she was away from her son. She didn't need to be with him to feel this. And I had her test it out. She could feel the constancy of the love while imagining that her son was at school eating lunch. She could feel it while thinking about herself going out to dinner with a friend. She could even feel it while imagining her son living with his own family many years from now."

"So she got it," I said. "She didn't have to be with her son in order to maintain that kind of connection! And you were right there with her. Not leading, but collaborating. I totally love it!"

Jill smiled widely. "That's what I love about this group! I can bring doubt and joy and success and you guys will get it!"

Jill's ability to recognize and share her Flow moment was beautiful. Once therapists learn to identify Flow, they capture it and want to celebrate. In Jill's experience, she got to it through following her curiosity about the book rather than coming into session with answers. Her curiosity began the session, and her trust that it would lead somewhere invited her to engage fully with Danielle. At the point when she identified that Danielle was feeling an emotion other than fear, Jill was totally in Flow and didn't even stop to double-check her words. She was in a state of resonance with Danielle.

Old Woman Time

As an occupational therapist, Tanya saw many patients a day. She was in high demand and had to call on a wide variety of skills to successfully help her patients in her private practice. Her patients had both physical ailments and psychological scars that prevented them from doing some of the basic things in life. They were disabled, bereaved, low on hope, and stubborn. And Tanya absolutely adored them.

In my online Artfix program, Tanya came to know just how much she adored her patients and what she needed to do for herself in order to let that love be received. In doing so, she was able to become unblocked in her therapeutic process and experience Flow at work.

As an artist, Tanya knew about Flow. She talked about it like it was candy. "When I'm painting, I get lost in color," she said. "I feel invincible, like I could fly with my own two wings. I lose track of time and end up painting all night. I don't get tired. I don't stop to eat. I just create. Those are the times when I feel I'm at my very best."

Before Artfix, Tanya hadn't thought that Flow could happen in other areas of her life besides her painting. She especially hadn't considered that it could happen at her job. Because she found painting so pleasurable, she would paint into the early morning, catch a few hours of sleep, and then go to the office. She was exhausted and wished she could feel more fulfilled at her job.

When she was asked, as part of the program, to find a Flow moment in her work with patients, she was surprised to find one fairly easily. Tanya recalled working with a woman in her eighties. The woman had recently lost her husband of 60 years to a long list of ailments, and she had come to occupational therapy because of her debilitating arthritis. She was wracked with grief, and Tanya found herself feeling immense compassion for her client. This kind of compassion wasn't a rare occurrence for Tanya, but she didn't often fully express the adoration and love she felt. Instead, she tried to keep herself emotionally controlled in an effort to maintain a sense of professionalism. She used her intellect to solve occupational problems and worked on her patients' muscles to make them suppler, but she didn't show love in the vibrant way that she expressed when painting. This intellectual stance was effective and important, but Tanya had been holding herself back from Flow. She had drawn the line between her art and her therapy and didn't trust herself to show up as an artist and immerse herself in moments of Flow with her clients.

But with this 80-year-old woman, Tanya let her love pour out for her patient. She reported that she couldn't believe how powerful it was. She massaged the woman's muscles, but it wasn't just massage—she was releasing the woman's pain. "I felt as if her wrinkled skin was the most beautiful thing I'd ever seen," she said. "And I told her. Can you believe I told her?!"

Tanya and her patient worked for the normal 45 minutes, "but it felt like forever. Time slowed, and each minute was so full it swelled and stretched the seconds. I was on old woman time and I absolutely loved it." When Tanya was done with the massage, she didn't want to stop; she wanted to give more. So she showed her client some movement exercises that could help with balance while they talked about children and marriage and life. The massage and exercises were nothing out of the ordinary for Tanya to offer her clients—it was the feeling of being her best self with this woman that was different. She let the woman know her at a different level and opened herself to a greater capacity for healing.

"I've learned I should be my natural self with clients," said Tanya after reflecting on this experience. "Some things weren't meant to be tamed. If I let my true essence come with me to work, I will serve others more fully, and I will be so much more satisfied in my work and life." As a result of realizing this, Tanya came up with ways that could support her creative Flow at work. She understood that our creative process is supported by our aliveness—our humanness. When we embody this, rather than compartmentalizing it, we are more likely to have moments of Flow. Tanya respected her creative process at work more, so she didn't compromise it by exhausting herself with painting all-nighters. She found a routine that worked better for both of her arts—painting and occupational therapy—and, in the end, felt more inspired in both realms.

She wrote this poem to capture her insights and experience during Artfix.

> Work "close in."
> Open your heart so it leads
> And the full contact of emotion
> Will jolt you and your client.
> Wake us up!
> Shake us up!
> The possibility of change will shower down
> And you and she will look at each other and marvel
> At the masterpiece you've created together.

Hallway Therapy

Terri was another wonderful participant in my online course, Artfix. She worked as a social worker in a community clinic in the city. She told this story to the group in response to an activity that invited the participants to celebrate moments of Flow.

Once a year, Terri's organization sponsored an outreach program that provided vaccinations to homeless children. Terri was stationed in the shelter where the vaccines were being administered. She was doing intake and tending to those in the waiting area when she heard screaming and crying coming from the back where the nurses were giving vaccines. One of the nurses stuck her head out and said to Terri, "We need your help here. She's out of control."

Terri went back to find a small girl, about eight, fighting for her life not to get a shot. Several adults, including the girl's mother, held her in a chair as one nurse tried to jab the girl quickly in the arm. They all looked at Terri. Someone said, "We just need another pair of hands."

Terri put her hands up as if to say, "No way. Not me," and instead said, "Give me a minute."

The adults let the girl go and Terri reached out her hand. She had the feeling that the nurses were rolling their eyes. "Bleeding heart social worker always has to make it so difficult," she thought she heard them saying under their breath. Terri had a flash of doubt interfere with her decision to get the girl out of this room. It would have been just as easy to assist them in holding the girl's other shoulder. The vaccine would have been given by now, and the girl would have been on her way out the door. But Terri had already acted on her decision and was walking out the door with the girl. "We'll be right back," she called over her shoulder.

Terri found a quiet hallway where she invited the girl to sit. They introduced themselves to each other. The girl was in fact eight, and her name was Maggie. Terri remembers consciously taking off her social worker hat and telling herself to just be with Maggie. They didn't talk about the vaccinations. They didn't talk about her living circumstances. They didn't even talk about feelings. They played patty cake and had thumb wars. They played rock-paper-scissors and Twenty Questions. Their time together lasted all of ten minutes, but Terri remembers it feeling like a delightful lunch break—relaxed and satisfying.

Before long, a nurse poked her head down the hallway. "We need you at the front room, Terri. More intakes have arrived."

Terri got up and reached for her new little friend, who took her hand again. This time they walked down the hall, back to the nurses in the vaccination room. "You ready now?" Terri asked gently. Maggie nodded, walked over to the chair, and got vaccinated without a wince.

Terri tells that story to herself on hard days. It helps her keep going despite doubts or frustrations. It's a moment she keeps in her back pocket for when she needs to be reminded about the rewards of the hard work she does. She remembers feeling totally activated, heart beating, breath fast, a warmth passing through her body. She remembers feeling compelled to just do something different, even if it was against the expectations of others. And best of all, she remembers those magical ten minutes of Flow in the hallway with Maggie, a client who needed her to be at her best.

Many therapists I work with do what Terri did and end up tucking Flow moments in a back pocket for times when the need for inspiration strikes. As a result, we are better equipped to navigate the difficult places in the therapeutic process. Flow moments support us and keep us engaged and enlivened by our work.

Summary

The fifth stage of the creative process, Flow, is marked by feelings of joy and ease. We can experience physical responses such as tingling and narrowed vision. We can feel like everything is going right and we are highly in sync with our client or our art. We get there by navigating the other stages and by being authentic, alive, and present. When we recognize the experience, we reap the rewards of hard work in the other stages of the creative process. While Flow is not the end goal of any creative endeavor, it certainly helps to reinforce the fact that difficult feelings such as doubt, anxiety, or fear are only one aspect of the creative process. As we collect experiences of Flow, we build greater resilience and trust in our work and creativity.

Questions to Ponder

1. What was a Flow experience that you can remember in your life? It could be a memory of a time when things seem to go right, or a peak experience where you felt jubilant and full of life. Write down a vivid description of your experience.
2. What conditions were present for this Flow experience?
3. Are there areas in your life that you experience Flow regularly?
4. What conditions are required for these Flow experiences to occur?
5. Who are you when you are your very best, most "self-actualized" self?
6. How can you bring that very best self into your work more reliably?
7. What changes might you have to make in order to cultivate the conditions that support your best self and thus your experience of Flow?
8. With whom can you share your Flow experiences ethically so that they are celebrated?
9. How would you like to have that person respond to your sharing so that your Flow moments are honored?

Art Invitations

Though you might have experienced Flow while engaging in any of the art activities from previous chapters, it is a wonderful thing to purposefully recognize the feeling of Flow and, in so doing, celebrate, honor, and cultivate more of these wonderful experiences. These art activities are designed to help you recognize Flow moments in your work.

Gratitude Tags

While therapy's primary aim is to assist clients in reaching their goals, we as therapists invariably benefit from the relationships.

We learn things from our clients that are personally and professionally invaluable. We experience Flow moments that enrich our lives. We get to witness human resilience and transformation from the front lines. In order to affirm your creativity and the peak experiences that you have with your clients, I suggest you start a collection of Gratitude Tags.

Here's what you need:

- Shipping tags (available in various sizes at office supply or craft stores)
- Markers
- Yarn or ribbon
- Optional: paint or colorful paper
- A special container to keep your tags in—jar, old cigar box, decorated shoe box.

Here's how:

1. **"Things I've learned" tags:** Think about specific things that you've learned from clients. Whether it was small (like a food to try) or bigger (like how going to a personal trainer could help depression), these lessons deserve to be remembered. As they happen during the week, write each one on the back of a blank tag. For example: "Thank you, DC, for introducing me to dried mango. It's my new favorite snack." "Thank you, JM, for helping me know more about yoga and how it can help with sleep problems."
2. **"Peak moments" tags:** Capture moments of Flow with a client or a group so that you can remember them. When a Flow moment happens, write it down on the back of a blank tag. Try to do it justice by being a bit poetic. As you are writing it, ask yourself, *What did I do to help make this moment happen?*
3. Writing on the tags may be plenty for you. You might also consider painting or collaging the tags to augment the writing.
4. Add a ribbon or colorful piece of yarn in the tag's hole.

5. Keep them safe. On a bad day, go through them and smile. When nearing burnout or faced with professional self-doubt, read them and remember how valuable your job is to yourself and to your clients.

Figure 7.1 Gratitude Tags (see color version in plate section)

The three gratitude tags shown represent valuable life lessons that each of these therapists learned from a client. Left: I wrote, "Thank you for teaching me that even sassiness can be part of a healing relationship." Middle: Susan wrote, "I am grateful for the privilege of accompanying you through your grief process following the sudden death of your sister." Right: Shelley wrote, "Thank you for reminding me that even in the darkest places, healing can happen."

Honoring Flow

When Flow happens, it is beautiful. It deserves an art activity all by itself.

Here's what you need:

- Cardboard or heavy paper
- Paint or other ways to add color.

Here's how:

1. Think of a time when you've felt a moment of Flow—when time slipped away and you felt like everything was going right. It might have been with a client, in a group, or during a yoga class. It could have been while you were making art (maybe one of the art invitations in this book). Relive that moment in your imagination and allow it to come to life again.

2. Using your art materials, represent the moment. It doesn't have to look like something specific; it can be abstract. Play with the color and texture to honor and intensify your representation. Just allow yourself the experience of immersing yourself in the creative process and celebrating the rewards of your art making.

3. Put up your art in a special place so that you can remember and honor your Flow moment.

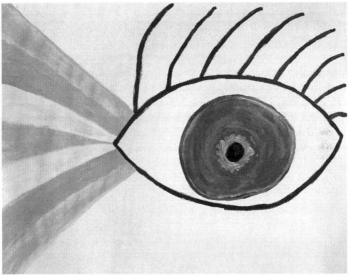

Figure 7.2 Carly's "Honoring Flow" (see color version in plate section)

Carly wanted to capture a new experience she'd started having as a result of learning to partner closely with her creative process. She said, "For me, Flow is that moment when I can capture the contradictions and see that integration out of the corner of my eye. I know now that if I follow this, it turns into something." She was excited to do this more in her work and in her personal life.

Figure 7.3 Ruth's "Honoring Flow" (see color version in plate section)

Ruth thinks about Flow as a pure experience. It reminds her of a time in her life when her children were young. "Thinking about them, the breathing in of their purity and goodness, is a place of bliss. It is where time stands still." She felt so connected. This happens for Ruth with other peoples' children and, sometimes, with clients. When it does, she decided she is going to honor it.

CONCLUSION

I'd like to close this book with a final invitation. It's a story about an instructional music clinic for middle-school students that I had the privilege of chaperoning in 2012. Rather than simply telling you the story, I'd like to invite you to come along with me—to imagine yourself as a participant in the audience. We can sit together, elbow to elbow, in the comfy auditorium seats.

Here we are, at the California State University–Sacramento Traditional Jazz Youth Band Festival, an annual event where elementary- through high-school bands receive live mentoring from professors and professional musicians. It's a marathon of sorts: multiple bands perform for various mentors in every room big enough to accommodate the musicians and their audiences. We, as viewers, have been most excited about the evening performance because we want to see the grand finale. This is the culminating concert where each band gets to showcase a piece, and then the professionals take the stage to close down the festival with their inspiring musical talent.

We are part of a proud audience. It consists mostly of parents and relatives of these aspiring young musicians and the young people themselves. They jostle their instruments as they listen, and as we sit among them, we feel the buzz of excitement. As each band finishes their showcase number, there are whistles and shouts that spur our feeling of being part of something special. Young people with passion are so alive, it feels contagious.

The amateur bands finish and international performer and recording artist Bob Draga takes the stage with the other guest musicians. You and I glance at one another with eyebrows raised. Each one of them must be exhausted. It's been a long weekend, they've mentored dozens of bands, and now, on this late Sunday night, they are about to give it their all. We listen intently. We feel captured and entranced, like the young musicians around us. We shout encouragement to the soloists and clap loudly to show our excitement for the band's renditions of *A Train, Georgia,* and *Take Five.*

Then Steve Roach, Dean of Music enters from stage right. He has a piece of paper in his hand and we settle in for what we think will be some teaching narrative about the pieces, the day, the band on stage. Instead, he reads the names of four teen sax players who have been picked for their shining performances during the instructional music clinics throughout the day. As he reads, he asks each kid to come up on stage. Three shiny new sax-playing kids rocket out of their seats. One has to be texted to come quickly. Once they gather, Dr. Roach asks dramatically, "Do you want to have your life changed today?" We clap and laugh because the kids show no hesitation. Of course they want to risk everything! They want to play music with this totally amazing professional jazz group in front of an audience of professional musicians, college professors, and scrutinizing peers to show us what they are made of.

We sit in the audience. Ruffled. Excited. Anxious.

I can read your thoughts. I'm feeling the same doubts. Was this guy asking way too much of these yet unformed teens? What about the pimply prepubescent baritone sax player? He's the youngest, but he'd been the most enthusiastic in his response. He's practically danced himself off the edge of the stage with excitement. But is he about to be embarrassed by his mediocrity? Will we have to shift from feasting on the music like it was a gourmet meal and instead laboriously pick out the edible parts in order to be a supportive audience? How is it going to feel as these young musicians honk through what they hope is good enough?

I'm not sure whether to be excited or scared. I can't decide if it is the greatest opportunity or an invitation for sure, ego-deflating failure. I want to protect the kids, and I want to encourage them. It's a bit white-knuckled here in these comfy seats at the end of a long night.

Are you with me? It's tense and worrisome, exciting and exhilarating. It might be a disaster. It might be fantastic. We just don't know. Can you imagine it—hoping and wanting the kids to feel good, to indeed have their lives changed, but secretly doubting that this could be even a remote possibility? They are beginners. They are not music savants. They are just cute, gangly kids willing to take a risk.

The moment comes when the sixth-grade bari sax player is cued to play his first 16-bar solo with the band. He had quickly scrawled some chord progressions on a few note cards before he came onstage and he's looking down at them spread before him on the floor. You and I and the rest of the audience mirror his hunched shoulders as he stands and strains to see the cards. Four bars into it, we are swept away on a tide of his passion. He's honked out two rhythm patterns that resonate with charisma and we are on our feet, hoarse from cheering, teary with amazement. He looks up at the audience for his next four bars and we see the twinkle in his eyes. He's with us in a full embodiment of jazz. He doesn't look down at his cards again, and as he completes the 16 bars, he reaches down and scoops up his note cards. While we jump up and down together, clapping between whistles, he throws the cards over his shoulder in a shower of celebration. The rain of scrawled paper makes us cheer even more.

Each of the other three sax players treats us to a similar experience. We are enthralled. At the end (which is a while because we don't want it to stop), Steve Roach comes up to each of the kids with a smile on his face. He shakes their hands. He applauds them and asks us to applaud some more. I'm certain his satisfied smile is saying, "See what happens when people take creative risks? They become the most incredible artists. Period."

It was a great show. It was a peak emotional experience for both the kids and the audience. I hope you enjoyed it as much as I did.

And I truly hope that, in even a small way, this book can be your invitation to take creative risks—to be brave, get up on stage, and see what you can do when you are spontaneous and fully immersed in the creative process of doing therapy. I hope that you can see in yourself what we got to see in the middle-school jazz players: that you are an artist and therapy is your art form. And I hope that you let yourself experience the possibility of throwing your notecards or your therapeutic protocols over your shoulder in a celebration of passion for your spontaneous, authentic, creative process.

I know, and I hope you do, too, that if I see my clients as artists, I see their tears as diamonds. If I see their crises as performance art, there is always an element that is beautiful. If I refuse to conclude how someone's struggle is going to play out, and instead see it one step at a time, one solo at a time, I often get my mind blown. If I believe in others because their creative potential is unlimited, I never collapse into hopelessness. And if I can show others my lens and invite them up on stage to participate, there could be a crescendo of applause and an experience that will change our lives for the better.

Appendix

ART IN GROUPS

"I have experienced creativity as a spirit that flies among people and things." Shaun McNiff (1998: p. 79). The exercises in this book are meant to be invitations to become more closely aligned with your creative process. They can be done in the cozy privacy of your office and shared with no one. They can also be done in groups—consultation, supervision, or otherwise. There is no wrong way, for sure. But I'd be remiss if I didn't talk further about the power of creativity in groups and why I think it is so wonderful for therapists to join together in this way. There are also some important considerations to make when you bring art into groups, and I'd like to pass on to you some of those ideas so that if you decide to start your own group, it can be nurturing and inspiring to all of your members.

In the chapter on Flow, I shared my memory of band camp and that incredible feeling of being a part of something bigger than myself. It filled me with hope and potential and trust in the process of collaboration. I also experienced this feeling in graduate school, in the art warehouse on campus. I was 24 years old with a bleached white shock of bangs falling from my otherwise shaved head, trying to look the part of an artist. What I didn't know until then: it's not about looks. It's about immersing oneself in the resonant buzz of the creative process and, in so doing, contributing to the creation of a common energy field.

The Collective Hum of Co-Creation

It was 3 a.m. We were bleary eyed and drunk on creative energy. The new Ani Difranco song floated down from the upstairs studios where one of the senior art students must still have been working. Downstairs, we packed away the clay in airtight bags. Our unfinished sculptures got wrapped in wet plastic, mummified with the promise of more work.

I shelved my project where I could find room. The drying shelves were packed full with works in progress. A small library of figures, stacked floor to ceiling, awaited their artists' return. Some were now abandoned and brittle. Bone-white dancers and terra cotta trees stood dusty and still with the expectation that someone would bring their inspiration to fire and glaze them.

All day, the metal ducting and high warehouse ceilings whirred with creative energy. We worked on the worn wooden slab tables, each enthralled by our own project and wrapped in the unified buzz of art making.

It didn't take me long to figure out that it was only the hardcore artists who logged these kinds of hours at the studio. And because I craved the long batches of time and wanted to eat art making instead of food, I decided I must be one of them. So I moved in. I had a locker where I kept tools and granola bars. I had a shelf of unfinished or drying sculptures. I was enrolled in various graduate-level classes: industrial art, mold making, mixed media survey. And, most importantly, I had the honor of being included in the all-night art-making sessions.

Sometimes we talked about personal issues. A lot of times we didn't talk at all. I don't remember the people, exactly. I just remember the womb-like feeling of being cradled in so much creativity—the union, the resonance, the result of a group of artists summoning a team of muses. It felt like some deeply hidden wound of mine was being stitched together. The collective hum of co-creation became something I craved, something I depended on.

Twenty-five years later, I still thrive on this sense of glorious creative synthesis when I am with a group that is engaged in art-making activities. It arrives quietly, like a bird alighting on a delicate branch. Much of the time it goes unnoticed because of its subtle hypnotic nature, until someone in the group steps out of the spellbound field of creativity to comment. Often, it's simply stated: "This is so wonderful," accompanied by a smile and a relaxed sigh. Sometimes it is questioned: "What is it that is so magic about making art in a group like this? Why can I create here and not alone in my own home?" Always, there is a declaration of gratitude: "I'm so happy to be here with all of you."

Powerful things happen when folks who are passionately committed to their art band together to form these enclaves. I love to visit artist collectives for this very reason. To inhabit their space feels like entering a hive. The creative buzz is tangible; the mess is purposeful; and the force of the artists' collective intention makes me feel braver—almost invincible.

Artists who join collectives are smart. They understand that if they work with others, their creative energy is pooled and the productivity increases exponentially. To be part of that pool is to be ultimately supported and fueled.

I love to watch and feel this dynamic during the workshops I facilitate for therapists. Even the newest artist can't spend very long hesitating when the rest of the group has taken a deep dive into to their creative discovery. The gentle tug of the creative hum inspires courage in even the hardcore lingerers. And it is inevitable that the group invites the novice creative explorer to take the plunge into the collaborative swirl of creative mess.

However, not all groups have this feel. Instead, there can be a sluggishness, like the passion is a bit stagnant, and in its place a sense of drag or dread has crept in. It is quite possible that caseload contributes to this feeling. Client symptom severity could also contribute. But caseload and symptom severity alone don't prohibit us from pooling our creative energy. It is more a matter of cultural tradition.

Historically, therapists have formed groups to contribute to our ongoing development. We recognize that we can't go it alone, and that isolation in this line of work can be a dangerous thing. But when therapists gather formally, we generally tend to pursue supervision, consultation, or education. In most supervision groups, we learn to address the clinical fires that need to be handled and get new ideas that are aimed at bettering our approaches with specific clients. At trainings and workshops, therapists gather to learn new techniques and theoretical approaches and to stay abreast of the latest research that will assist them in delivering quality services to clients. Supervision, consultation, and education play important roles in our ongoing development as therapists, but these groups are far cries from the fertile ground of the artist collective.

There are also occasions when therapists gather informally for support and camaraderie. These lunch dates or between-session conversations are great ways to connect and ward off the blues of working in isolation. When these connections happen, sometimes we complain about our clients and commiserate about the difficulties of our work. Other times we talk about our marketing issues or caseloads or other aspects of the job that weigh on us. Validation from friends who understand is crucial for our well-being, but these encounters often lack the kind of creative collaboration and encouragement of risk taking that art groups provide.

Artist collectives show us a glimpse of the missing piece in our group experiences as therapists. Beyond our established ways of meeting, art groups can provide us with a key to cultivating creative resilience in the face of our traditional therapist culture, which tends to foster negativity and doubt. In art groups, we can be imperfectly human and get excited about the happy accidents and the ugly messes we make. There is freedom, connection, and vital expression.

Meet the Fluffers

For the last seven years, I have had the distinct privilege of being a part of a therapist art collective. Belinda, Susan, Eileen, Kate, Leslie, and Jamie were participants in my Professional

Journaling workshop in 2008. When they completed a wonderful ten weeks of altered book journaling about their experiences as therapists, they didn't want it to end. Belinda started suggesting ways that the group could keep going. They were figuring out meeting locations and how they could make it work. I grappled with my ethics for about half a second and then piped in, "I want to meet with you guys, too. But I don't want to facilitate—I want to be in your group!" They whooped and clapped, and eight years later we still meet once a month for four hours to make art together. For all of us, those four hours serve as reconnection and revival, and help us stir the pot of inspiration so that we can thrive in our lives and work.

We've evolved over the years, and we've done many different art-making activities in various group configurations. Overarching is our sense that we are an artist's collective. We show up and do our work not only for ourselves, but for the greater whole. We each understand that the environment in which we create is as much a priority as the activity of creating. In order to have this remain a constant, the group had to set up some important conditions to start with and to uphold along the way. I'd like to share them as guidelines and inspiration for Creativity as Co-Therapist groups to form everywhere.

The Environment

My studio was the natural meeting place for our group. It was midway between various resident cities and had already proved convenient for everyone. I also had large table space that could accommodate all seven of us comfortably. At first, folks wanted to pay me for supplies. I wanted to shift the group from this mindset to a more collaborative one, so I suggested that we follow a model that I had enjoyed as a child.

When I was four years old, my mother and brother didn't have much money, so buying things new or even used was out of the question. There was a thrift store that we used to visit to get most of our clothes and toys. The thrift store was truly a community center; there was a section of the store where we could exchange our toys or clothes. I remember arriving at the store with an old stuffed animal and a pair of shoes I'd out-grown, adding these items to the bin, and feeling thrilled to leave with a bigger, gently used pair of shoes and a new-to-me stuffed animal. No one monitored our exchanges for fairness. No one questioned our frequency. It was easy and friendly and fundamentally supportive.

The Fluffers and I have this kind of arrangement. They arrive at my studio and unload their exchange items into the middle of the table. Sometimes we use those items during our meeting; often I add them to the art supply shelves for later use. Susan brings baby wipes every time she comes. Belinda likes to bring paint and brushes. A couple of times, a few of them have wanted to add a $20 bill to the pile to cover something that the group may not have thought of. It all works out, each person adding to the collective in their own thoughtful way. No tabs, no tallies, just generosity and gratitude.

The environment can be structured in any way, but keep in mind the essential message: shared space in which art making can happen is powerful and exhilarating.

The Goal

If it isn't consultation, and it isn't education, and it isn't therapy—then why do we meet? I asked this question at our Fluffer meeting recently. I wanted to know: after all these years, what keeps us coming back?

While it was hard to articulate, we all agreed that being seen and known to one another was the main goal of the group. Our art facilitates this because of the visually expressive dimension that it brings to our sharing. Belinda summed it up like this: "Art doesn't lie. If you don't think and just let it come through you, it's all right there." We all value the act of uncovering layers that our group and our art provide. It's what has kept us going for such a long time.

Early on, we engaged in various art activities that helped this process happen. For a whole year, we explored the metaphor of a doorway in our art. We talked about the kinds of masks we wore for our clients, and what went on behind the scenes for each of us. We made art about what our clients saw and how this compared to what we saw in each other. Working with the doorway metaphor was a powerful self-reflective activity, and it also served the group by illuminating multiple layers beyond what we already knew about each other.

One of my most cherished treasures is an altered book in which each group member created a page for me. We filled another year with this art activity, where we passed our books around and, during each meeting, added a page to a group member's book. The page was a collage about how we saw that person, what their special strengths were, what we valued about them. It is amazing to look back at this book. The layers of my friends' knowledge about me is uncanny. Even my color palette and favorite words are captured.

It is a rare and wonderful experience to feel known—without being judged—by other therapists. The layers of understanding go deep because we each know the role of therapist and how it adds to the rich challenges of being human. Jamie recalled, "Hearing everybody talk about their art, I stopped pathologizing myself. I tend to doubt myself as a therapist, and it's the same with my art. To see other's openness made me feel more okay in a very tangible way." The art gave us an inroad both in content (through the doorway activity, for example) and because of the supportive conditions required of an art group of this nature.

Creating an Artist's Culture

Our group cultivates the feeling of an innovation-focused artist's culture. It needs to feel safe and supportive on a dual level. With the art, we need a sense of freedom and openness to experiment with materials. With the therapy aspect, it is essential that each group member eschews the judgmental nature of our therapist's culture and instead brings to one another the deep compassion that we know so well from our work with clients.

Necessary Conditions

Value Diversity

When seasoned therapists and novice therapists come together in a collaborative way, a rich depth of sharing occurs. It is wonderful to hear novice therapists sigh with relief when they hear that experienced therapists can have the same feelings of doubt or overwhelm as they do. Seasoned therapists visibly soften when they are able to talk about their vulnerabilities and take off the suit of proficiency that they've had to wear for so long.

In our own Fluffers group, I'm the youngest chronologically and find there is such a rich exchange about being a therapist (and a woman) across the lifespan. We have members in their sixties and seventies who bring a perspective that I value immensely. We can be linked together in our common role as therapists, and honor the diversity that comes in many different forms.

Get Personal

As therapists, we constantly monitor how much self-disclosure to bring into session. We have a professional filter that serves as a necessary therapeutic tool. In an art group, that filter no longer serves. The art will automatically reveal feelings and unconscious expressions that are way beyond that professional filter. So it is much better to cultivate a safe environment where each group member allows herself to get personal. It requires courage to be imperfect and vulnerable with others. Sometimes this comes naturally, and sometimes the group has to intentionally invite it through activities and conversations. Some of the art activities in this book ("What Blocks You?" from Chapter 5 and "Gratitude Tags" from Chapter 7, for instance) would be a great start. I've described some additional art activities at the end of this appendix.

Permissiveness

Whatever the activity the group chooses, there has to be an atmosphere of permissiveness. When we enter an artist collaborative, art making and mess making are going on all around. This same invitation to "do your own thing" has to be conscientiously reinforced. Group members should remind each other, "There is no wrong way."

In our Fluffers group, there have been times when each of us just didn't feel like making art. I've sat in many a group meeting and just knitted and talked while the others engaged with the art activity. Eileen likes to bring cookies and brownies to decorate. Leslie works on handwork, quilting, and sewing when she's not up for the activity. Jamie has spent many groups just sitting with us while she ponders what's next for her art.

There are messy times, and glitter times, and difficult, ugly times in all of our art. Whatever we bring to the group, it needs to be honored and accepted. There are few places in the world where we can feel this level of permission, and a therapist art group is a perfect and invaluable place for allowing each member to do what they need and want to do. This culture of permissiveness strengthens the group commitment. It invites members to show up no matter what, which reinforces each individual's commitment to the group and her own creative process.

Curiosity and Respect

If we bring an artist's eye to any situation, we bring infinite curiosity, which is really the key to permissiveness. Curiosity is so strong in an artist that it overrides judgment. If each group member can intentionally choose curiosity over evaluation (of themselves and others), the group will thrive.

Asking questions that are process-related rather than product-related can get to a place of curiosity rather than evaluation. The questions, "How did you make that?" or "How did that feel for you to make?" ask about a person's art process. In contrast, the questions, "What is that?" or "What does that mean?" inquire about the person's art product. To be curious about the art process is to honor the artist's experience and to invite the kind of personal sharing that the group needs.

Don't Do Consultation

While it can be tempting to take advantage of the time with other therapists and talk about clients, consultation detracts from the art activities and the group process. When we go into consultation mode, we immediately put a therapist hat on and see things through that clinical filter. The group's purpose is to encourage vulnerability and sharing outside our clinical role.

That said, I think it is invaluable to talk about our personal experience as therapists. Sometimes that means talking about specific interactions with clients, but it is in the service of sharing, not for getting ideas or feedback on our clinical approach with a specific client. There have been times in our Fluffers group when each of us has struggled significantly in our roles for various reasons. When we've shared those moments and really opened ourselves to being seen by the other group members who understand the struggle because of their own work as therapists, it has deepened our connections with each other.

Have Fun and Laugh

Our roles and responsibilities can be very serious and intense. Our art making about those experiences can also be somber. While it's important to honor this seriousness, it is also wonderful to share laughter and have fun. Besides, a sense of play is such important fuel for creativity. Bring lightness, silliness, and exaggeration into the group and the art work. Giggle with one another. Tell ridiculous stories and have conversations that might not happen in a more "professional" environment.

At the end of every art group, The Fluffers literally "fluff our auras." Early on, Eileen taught us something she'd learned in a dance class and we giggled about it for a long time. We ended up thinking it was so fun and funny that it ended up being something we did before saying goodbye after each group meeting. We all stand up around the table and "fluff" the air around our bodies. We look ridiculous. We smile. We each go home renewed for another month of hard and rewarding work.

Summary

Banding together as artists can be life- and career-sustaining. The collective effort toward creating for the sake of being seen and known is extraordinarily powerful. When we get swept up in this creative buzz, we breathe life into our work as therapists. When we intentionally practice navigating the creative process and find support in doing so, we grow our capacity to heal and help. Many of the questions, art activities, and guidelines in this book can be used in forming Creativity as Co-Therapist Groups. I also facilitate many different therapist groups online and as private retreats. Please see the Resources at the back of this book for more information.

Group Art Invitations

Here are a couple of art activities specifically designed to help a Creativity as Co-Therapist Group when it is first starting out.

What's in Your Heart?

It is seldom that we can really share the doubt or pain that we carry for clients at times. This art activity is aimed at giving group members permission to share the layered experience of their work.

Here's what you need:

- Collage materials—magazines for images
- An enlarged image of an anatomical heart, preferably a line drawing, which can be found online and then enlarged at your local copy center
- Glue
- Scissors.

Here's how:

1. Cut images from magazines that capture your answer to the question, "What resides in your heart as a result of being a therapist?" These can be concrete images (both positive and negative). They can also be senses or abstractions like texture and color, cut from partial images.
2. Glue your images onto the outline of a heart.
3. You may wish to color or paint over these lines or remaining shapes to complete the collage.
4. Share your answers to these questions with your group.
   - What words go with each collage image?
   - What is surprising for you to see?
   - What are you curious about?
   - How does your heart feel now that you can see it outside of yourself?
   - What does your heart invite you to think about going forward?
5. As a group, validate common experiences that you heard when sharing your art. Talk about how you can support one another in these common experiences.
6. As a group, validate the depth that the art brought to your experience and make a commitment to continue this kind of collective experience.

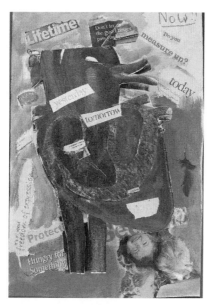

Figure 8.1 Belinda's "What's in Your Heart?"

Belinda said, "My very first supervisor warned me that I couldn't keep taking it all home with me or I would die in this profession. My heart shows how much I still take home after all these years. Doing art with this group, I have realized how undernourished I was."

Figure 8.2 Kate's "What's in Your Heart?"

Kate shared that she felt reconnected to herself as a result of this art activity. When she shared it with us, she said, "There are heavy things in my heart, but when I show them and share them I instantly feel lighter."

Altered Books

This activity took my group an entire year. We worked in each other's books, completing one page per meeting.

Here's what you need:

- A hardcover book that can be altered with paint and art
- Paint
- Collage materials.

Here's how:

1. Exchange books so that you are working on someone else's book, not your own. Glue a few pages together so that you are working on a thick spread of two pages.
2. Using any kind of art materials that you would like, represent aspects of the group member whose book you are working in. Think of the colors that represent that person for you. Use phrases that they say. Represent things about them that you admire.
3. When you are done with that spread, present it to the owner as if you are giving a gift. Talk about what you thought of while making the spread. Show that person what you see and what you value by sharing the art that you made.
4. Continue to exchange books for each group meeting until every group member has contributed to each group member's book.
5. In your own book, work on the cover. Have the cover depict the experience that you've had in giving and receiving these pages.

Figure 8.3 A Page in My Book

"When I look at this page, it shows me the seed of a friendship that has grown into a lifeline. The activity helped us bond and it documents a precious memory. It's a tangible memento of a very important part of my life."

Figure 8.4 A Page in Belinda's Book (see color version in plate section)

"It felt like a precious gift to receive something from each person and to see how different we all are in the things that we do. There was such sweetness and creativity and thoughtfulness that went into each page. I'll treasure my book and the experience of making one for each person in the group for years to come."

RESOURCES

If you would like to be inspired by more art activities, receive additional ideas for navigating the creative process, and get connected to other like-minded therapists, please visit my website at www.innercanvas.com. The trainings mentioned in this book can all be found on my site. You can find additional materials, including video demonstrations for many of the art invitations contained in this book. I hope to see you there!

For art supplies, I recommend the following stores:

Blick Art Materials (www.dickblick.com)

Utrecht Art (www.utrechtart.com)

Michael's (www.michaels.com).

Pop-Up Template

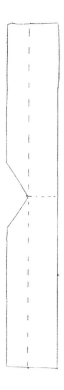

Figure 9.1 Pop-Up Template

Directions:

Copy this template so that it fits on an 8.5″ x 11″ piece of paper.
Print it out. Cut out and trace onto a heavy piece of paper.
Fold on the dotted lines and tape into the crease of a folded
piece of paper or book.
Glue images onto the part of the pop-up that is not taped.
For a video that explains and demonstrates the use of a pop-up,
please visit www.innercanvas.com/creativity-cotherapist.

REFERENCES

Art Institute of Chicago (2007). *Cezanne to Picasso*, exhibit brochure.
Retrieved from www.artic.edu/aic/exhibitions/picasso/themes.
html#about (accessed July 4, 2015).

Baldwin, M. (1987). "Interview with Carl Rogers." In *The Use of Self in
Therapy* (pp. 29–39). New York: Haworth.

Boston Museum of Science (n.d.). "Renaissance Man." Retrieved from
http://legacy.mos.org/leonardo/bio.html (accessed July 4, 2015).

Cameron, J. (1992). *The Artist's Way: A Spiritual Path to Higher Creativity*.
Los Angeles, CA: Jeremy P. Tarcher/Perigee.

Condivi, A. (2007). *The Life of Michelangelo*, trans. Charles Holroyd.
London: Anthene Pallas.

Csikszentmihalyi, M. (1996). *Flow: The Psychology of Discovery and
Invention*. New York: HarperCollins.

Duncan, B. L., Miller, S. D., Wampold, B. E., and Hubble, M. A. (eds.)
(2010). *The Heart and Soul of Change: Delivering what Works in
Therapy* (2nd edn.). Washington, DC: American Psychological
Association.

Godin, S. (2012). *The Icarus Deception: How High will you Fly?* (Kindle edn.)
New York: Portfolio/Penguin. Retrieved from www.amazon.com.

Goldberg, N. (2014). *Living Color*. New York: Abrams.

Harriss, J. A. (March 2001). Master class. *Smithsonian Magazine*.
Retrieved from www.smithsonianmag.com/arts-culture/master-
class-69130767/?no-ist (accessed October 6, 2015).

Kelley, T. and Kelley, D. (2013). *Creative Confidence: Unleashing the
Creative Potential Within us All*. New York: Crown Business.

Kelly, E. and Kelly, E. W. (2007). *The Irreducible Mind: Toward a Psychology
for the Twenty-First Century*. Maryland: Rowan and Littlefield.

Kohut, H. (1984). *How Does Analysis Cure?* Chicago: University of Chicago Press.

Kottler, J. A. and Carlson, J. (2014). *On Being a Master Therapist: Practicing what you Preach.* Hoboken, NJ: Wiley.

Kreuger, A. (2010). "15 Life-Changing Inventions that were Created by Mistake." *Business Insider,* November 16. Retrieved from www.businessinsider.com/these-10-inventions-were-made-by-mistake-2010-11?op=1&IR=T (accessed July 4, 2015).

Lamott, A. (1995) *Bird by Bird: Some Instructions on Writing and Life.* New York: Anchor.

Langer, E. J. (2005). *On Becoming an Artist: Reinventing yourself through Mindful Creativity.* New York: Ballantine.

McNiff, S. (1992). *Art as Medicine: Creating a Therapy of the Imagination.* Boston, MA: Shambhala.

McNiff, S. (1998). *Trust the Process: An Artist's Guide to Letting Go.* Boston, MA: Shambhala.

Makan, K. (2013). "My Dark Materials: The Music of Depression." *The New York Times,* January 15. Retrieved from http://opinionator. blogs.nytimes.com/2013/01/15/the-music-of-depression (accessed July 4, 2015).

Maslow, A. (1959). "Creativity in Self-Actualizing People." In H. Anderson (ed.), *Creativity and its Cultivation* (pp. 88–91). New York: Harper & Row.

Nachmanovitch, S. (1990). *Free Play: Improvisation in Life and Art.* New York: Tarcher.

Norcross, J. C. (2010). "The Therapeutic Relationship." In B. L. Duncan, S. D. Miller, B. E. Wampold, and M. A. Hubble (eds.), *The Heart and Soul of Change: Delivering what Works in Therapy* (2nd edn.). Washington, DC: American Psychological Association.

O'Donohue, J. (2008). "For the Artist at the Start of the Day." *To Bless the Space between us: A Book of Blessings.* New York: Doubleday.

Orlinsky, D. E. and Rønnestad, M. H. (2005). *How Psychotherapists Develop: A Study of Therapeutic Work and Professional Growth.* Washington, DC: American Psychological Association.

Tharp, T. (2003). *The Creative Habit: Learn It and Use It for Life: A Practical Guide.* New York: Simon & Schuster.

Yalom, I. (2015). "A Conversation with Dr. Irv Yalom." Palo Alto, CA: The Center for the Studio of Group Psychotherapy.

Zervos, C. (1952). "Conversation with Picasso." In B. Ghiselin (ed.), *The Creative Process: A Symposium* (pp. 55–60). Berkeley, CA: Regents of the University of California.

INDEX